HOW GOOD ARE SCHOOL GARDENS?

HOW GOOD ARE SCHOOL GARDENS?

EXPLORING THE HOLISTIC BENEFITS OF SCHOOL GARDEN EXPERIENCES

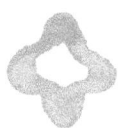

EMMA DERAINNE

Praise for *How Good are School Gardens?*

This more than just a book; it is a call to action. Emma's passionate advocacy for school gardens is contagious. *How Good are School Gardens?* is a vital resource for educators, parents and anyone interested in the intersection of education, wellbeing and the environment.

Margherita Ghezzi, Author, Program Coordinator, Education, Western Sydney University Online

How Good are School Gardens? offers a clear framework and reflections to help you set up or revive your school garden for success and sustainability. Based upon Emma's own experience and research into school gardens, this book is as practical as it informative.

Jennie Hodges, Nature-based Pediatric Occupational Therapist

Through a deep understanding of the transformative potential of school gardens, Emma Derainne illuminates how these spaces can nurture not only a connection to nature but also emotional resilience and healing. Emma's insights into the role school gardens play in fostering a sense of belonging, safety and emotional regulation are truly profound. This book is a must-read for anyone looking to create environments that support the holistic wellbeing of students.

Lisa Henderson, Teacher, School Guidance Counsellor, Trauma Researcher

How Good Are School Gardens? is a voice from teachers for teachers. The book offers practical insights into the benefits of outdoor learning for students with diverse needs. Emma beautifully captures how school gardens foster sensory engagement, social skills and emotional growth, making it a perfect tool for teachers looking to create inclusive, hands-on learning environments.

Emma A., Special Education Teacher

Published in 2024 by Amba Press, Melbourne, Australia
www.ambapress.com.au

© Emma Derainne 2024

All rights reserved. No part of this book may be reproduced or transmitted in any form or by any means, electronic or mechanical, including photocopying, recording or by any information storage and retrieval system, without prior permission in writing from the publisher.

Cover design: Tess McCabe
Internal design: Amba Press
Editor: Brooke Lyons

ISBN: 9781923215429 (pbk)
ISBN: 9781923215436 (ebk)

A catalogue record for this book is available from the National Library of Australia.

CONTENTS

About the Author		ix
Acknowledgements		xi
Introduction		1
One	Go Kick a Ball: The current state of children and nature	7
Two	Billy the Kid: Why are school gardens important?	27
Three	The Venus Flytrap: Meaning-making in the school garden	41
Four	Nurturing Resilience: Stressors and the school garden	55
Five	Guardians of Growth: The role of passionate teachers and enthusiastic supporters	67
Six	Growing Together: Peer-to-peer connection	81
Seven	Fairy Therapy: Emotional transformation in the school garden	95
Eight	Sir Worms-a-Lot: Supporting environmental sustainability	113
Nine	Roots of Connection: The holistic benefits of school gardens	131
Conclusion		149
References		159

ABOUT THE AUTHOR

Emma Derainne is a teacher. With a diverse career spanning early childhood education and primary school teaching across Australia, Asia and Europe, Emma brings a wealth of experience and perspectives to her work.

Currently serving as the Program Coordinator for Early Childhood Education and Food and Nutrition Sciences at Federation University Online, Emma is dedicated to shaping the future of education through innovative curriculum development and pedagogical practices.

Emma's commitment to excellence in teaching has been recognised through various accolades, including being a finalist in the Regional Universities Network Teaching and Learning Awards in 2024. Her passion for presenting and sharing knowledge was celebrated with a People's Choice Award at the Federation University Partnership Conference in 2024 and a Dean's Award in 2020 for Leadership and Management in Education, affirming her impact and influence within the education community.

Emma is a bilingual and bicultural author. With an Associate Fellowship (Indigenous Knowledges) from the Queensland Academy of Learning and Teaching, Emma brings a culturally responsive approach to her work, ensuring that school gardens serve as inclusive, accessible and empowering spaces for all students.

Emma's academic pursuits have led her to produce a research thesis and submit journal articles as a higher degree research student of the University of Queensland – ranked number one in Australia for Food Sciences and Technologies.

Through her extensive experience, dedication to excellence and unwavering passion for education, Emma continues to place the voices of teachers, parents, students and community members at the centre of school garden research and authorship. Emma hopes that *How Good are School Gardens?* will inspire people worldwide to get involved in and harness the potential of school gardens through their multifaceted meaning as transformative learning spaces.

ACKNOWLEDGEMENTS

Firstly, I extend my deepest gratitude to my children, Arthur and Oliver. Your presence in school gardens transformed my journey as a teacher, reshaping my perceptions and experiences. Interacting with you within those green spaces influenced the meaning that I attribute to school gardens, and I am endlessly thankful for that.

To my partner, Anthony, your unwavering support sustained me throughout the writing process of this book. Thank you for the countless cups of tea and for clearing away the tea circles that amassed around my computer like a protective fort. Your patience and encouragement were invaluable.

To my parents, Frances and Stephen, thank you for instilling in me a love for nature and a deep appreciation for the simple beauty of our world. I probably could have done without the brown snake in our letterbox on the farm as I collected our post, but nonetheless, your guidance and nurturing allowed my curiosity to flourish, shaping the person I am today.

To my siblings, Luke and Courtney, thank you for being my childhood companions in mischief and adventure. Our shared experiences, from mango throwing to bull-ant races, laid the foundation for my enduring passion for nature.

To my friends, your unwavering support and encouragement sustained me through moments of doubt and exhaustion. Whether through late-night monologue audio message recordings or 4am nature walks to just 'be', your presence reminded me of my courage, passion and purpose.

To my mentors, I appreciate your support. Thanks also to my publishing team: Alicia, Tess and Brooke.

And finally, but certainly not least, I extend my heartfelt thanks to all the mentors, students, parents, teachers, carers and community members involved in school gardens worldwide. Your dedication to these green spaces is crucial, and your collective efforts are shaping a brighter future for generations to come. Together, we affirm the importance of school gardens and the profound impact they have on education and community. Thank you for your commitment and contributions. We are truly indebted to you all.

INTRODUCTION

My name is Emma and I'm passionate about school gardens.

I'm also passionate about teaching. Like many other educators, it's more than a job for me; it's a vocation. I believe teaching is about sharing time, knowledge and experiences with children and young people, helping them to see and understand the world in their unique ways. My 20-plus-year career in early childhood and primary education has always been driven by a deep interest in how children perceive their surroundings. I firmly believe that there is much adults can learn from young people's perspectives and experiences.

In my current role as a program coordinator I focus on integrating holistic learning approaches such as school gardens into the curriculum. Over the years I have developed and implemented various educational programs that emphasise experiential learning, sustainability and community engagement. I get so much satisfaction from sharing my knowledge and enthusiasm with other educators, guiding them to incorporate school gardens into their teaching practices to enhance students' health, learning and wellbeing.

The topic of school gardens became significant to me when I met a student named Billy.

I was teaching in a classroom of five- to six-year-olds when I asked, 'Where do tomatoes come from?' Billy raised his hand and proudly voiced, 'From the supermarket!' At first, I thought Billy might be trying to make his classmates laugh (he had a tendency to do this – which was both endearing and annoying). But, worse, I then realised that Billy was deadly serious. He didn't know that tomatoes grew from the soil. I looked around the classroom and there were many other blank faces. No-one knew. I was shocked. Flabbergasted. And sure, this was an inner-city school, where most of the children lived in apartments, many without even a balcony to bask in the joy of a few potted plants. But in that moment, I felt very alone, very guilty and very responsible. We had failed Billy. More importantly, despite all my good intentions and pro-environmentalist behaviours, *I* had failed Billy.

It was a call to action. Billy needed me. *All* the Billys needed me.

I realised that, in our modern society, children are increasingly disconnected from nature. Technology has been invited into our homes, with children spending more time on 'devices' than any other generation. We live in more urbanised environments and have more structured lifestyles. We want to give our children the 'best' opportunities – to play the cello, take high-diving lessons and excel academically. So, we run our children around to various extracurricular activities with the goal of fulfilling them culturally, physically and intellectually. Through this blur, we have become used to the detachment from nature, and from each other.

This realisation prompted me to start researching school gardens. I soon found myself on a journey of discovery where I learned how crucial gardens are in schools. They offer myriad diverse benefits that go far beyond nutritional advantages. School gardens create dynamic learning environments that extend beyond traditional classroom settings, providing students with hands-on experiences in sustainability, biodiversity and environmental stewardship. School gardens can serve as therapeutic spaces, offering sensory fulfilment, promoting physical activity and supporting students to develop practical skills. Involving students in a school garden helps them understand the origins of their food, and fosters a sense of responsibility towards nature.

The therapeutic and sensory benefits of school gardens can be especially beneficial for students with special needs. The tactile engagement with plants and soil can be incredibly soothing and grounding. School gardens also promote physical activity. Engaging in gardening requires physical effort, such as digging, planting and weeding, which helps to improve students' overall fitness and health.

School gardens also play a significant role in developing practical skills. They teach valuable life skills, from growing and harvesting plants to understanding seasonal cycles and ecological relationships. These skills contribute to greater self-sufficiency and a deeper appreciation for nature, equipping students with knowledge and abilities that can be applied in various aspects of their lives. Additionally, school gardens enhance emotional and social wellbeing. They encourage peer-to-peer connections and improve student-teacher relationships. By providing a safe and secure environment for students to explore, learn and interact, school gardens foster a sense of community and belonging. These connections and relationships are vital for students' overall development and wellbeing.

The educational outcomes of integrating garden activities into the curriculum are substantial. Gardens serve as living laboratories where subjects such as science, maths and art come to life through real-world applications. This hands-on approach can deepen students' understanding and retention of academic concepts, making learning more engaging and effective. For instance, students might learn about plant biology by observing and tending to plants in the garden, or they might understand mathematical concepts through measuring and planning garden plots. These practical applications of academic subjects can make learning more relevant and exciting for students.

School gardens also promote community engagement. They can become hubs for community involvement, bringing together students, teachers, parents and local residents. This collective effort not only enhances the garden's success but also strengthens community bonds and encourages a shared investment in educational outcomes. Community members can contribute their knowledge, skills and resources to support the garden, creating a sense of ownership and pride. This engagement can also provide students with opportunities to learn from different perspectives and experiences, enriching their educational journey. This is particularly important for communities with a rich agricultural or cultural heritage, with skills that can be passed from generation to generation.

This book offers encouragement and support to integrate school gardening into your educational practice. These spaces support students' holistic development. By creating interactive and inclusive learning experiences, school gardens cater to diverse student needs and promote a well-rounded educational approach. The impact of these gardens extends far beyond the nutritional benefits of the produce they yield. They contribute to student growth, development and wellbeing in a multifaceted way, encompassing therapeutic, physical, practical, emotional, social and academic dimensions.

By fostering a deeper connection to nature and providing a hands-on learning environment, school gardens offer students opportunities to develop important life skills, build meaningful relationships and engage with their communities. They help students understand the broader ecological and social systems they are a part of, instilling a sense of responsibility and stewardship. In this way, school gardens not only enhance educational outcomes but also contribute to the development of well-rounded, conscientious individuals who are prepared to make positive contributions to their communities and the world at large.

This book provides practical guidance, real-life examples and reflective prompts that will help you integrate school gardening into your teaching practice. It emphasises the importance of understanding the sociocultural context of your school and tailoring garden programs to meet specific needs. The book offers strategies for community engagement, tips for maintaining safety and security, and ideas for cross-curricular learning. It encourages you to celebrate your successes, seek support when needed, and continuously adapt your approach to make the most of your school garden.

To get the most from this book, I encourage you to adopt a reflective and open-minded approach. The book is structured to guide you through various aspects of establishing and maintaining a school garden, from initial planning to integrating garden activities into the curriculum. Each chapter includes journal prompts designed to encourage reflection and planning. I suggest you keep a dedicated journal to work through these prompts, record your thoughts and develop actionable plans.

I hope you will approach this book with curiosity, flexibility and a commitment to continuous improvement. School gardens are not one-size-fits-all; they require adaptation to the unique sociocultural contexts of each school. By engaging deeply with the content, reflecting on your practices and actively seeking ways to incorporate garden-based learning, you can create enriching, sustainable and impactful educational experiences for your students.

So, let's take a walk down the garden path together. I hope, by the end of this book, you will join me in exclaiming: 'How good are school gardens?'

ONE

GO KICK A BALL

THE CURRENT STATE OF CHILDREN AND NATURE

'Go and kick a ball outside.' This is something that parents all over the world say to their children. Or at least, it used to be. However, in modern society, simply 'going and kicking a ball outside' is not as easy as it once was. Quite a lot of children don't have immediate access to outside spaces in close proximity to where they live. This is because most of the population now lives in urbanised settings where green spaces are rare. Childhood is now spent predominantly in non-nature environments. By 2030, 60 per cent of the global population will live in urban centres (Knorr et al., 2018). As cities worldwide grow and land becomes valuable for housing and industry, the possibility for green spaces decreases. The tipping point for urban living was in 2007, which was the first year that a higher percentage of the population lived in urban, rather than rural, areas (United Nations, 2018). The world is on a trajectory to have more urban populations than rural populations, with a predicted urban population of 7 billion by 2050. This means that more children will grow up in urban settings – so the 'go kick a ball' solution of the 70s, 80s and 90s becomes challenging for children.

The realities for today's children

If you live in or near a large city, when you think about dense housing your mind may go directly to those very-high-density public housing apartment blocks where children don't have any outdoor space. They live in apartments that don't even have a balcony. While there are more children living in apartments or smaller urban dwellings such as these due to current cost-of-living pressures, there are other examples of children living with limited green spaces all around us. Think about those expansive housing estates with names such as 'Park Haven', 'Green Meadows', 'Destiny', 'Harmony' or 'Infinity'. Ironically, many of the streets in these estates are named after the types of trees that had to be cut down to make way for the houses: 'Paperbark Court', 'Eucalyptus Terrace' or 'Birch Tree Way'. The houses are ticky-tacky, stacked in little rows of two by ten. In the housing developments that are being constructed now, many of the 'house-and-land' packages have standalone houses on blocks of just 400 square metres or less. Small block sizes create highly dense areas. The expansive blocks of land that were common in the 80s are now the only ones that are over 800 square metres, and many have been sub-divided and sold off to construct duplexes – stuffing more people in and further decreasing the green space.

It's almost impossible to think that you could buy an 800-square-metre block for your house now. Therefore, even children who *do* live in houses have very small outdoor spaces at home. In many cases the house itself fills most of the footprint of a smaller block space. It reminds me of that song by Malvina Reynolds about little boxes on the hillside, made of ticky-tacky, that all look the same. Are you the pink one, the green one, the blue one or the yellow one? In most cases there's only a small strip of space left for outdoor play. And, particularly in Australia, often that outdoor space is taken up by entertaining areas, which are mostly paved, or pools – because, well, Bob and Jin have a pool, so we want one, too. 'The kids will love it.' Consequently, we are restricting ourselves and, our children from enjoying close or immediate access to a grassed space to, as we say, 'kick a ball around'.

With the increased cost of living and house prices soaring, many families can't afford to live in houses with even a small backyard. The ideal of backyard cricket in large, expansive spaces is really a thing of the past. So it's not as easy to say to children, 'Go outside and kick a ball around.' It's really not their fault they don't have outdoor space to enjoy. And yet, I've heard many older folks in supermarket queues give out free advice to parents indicating that children are in some way responsible for their lack of ball kicking. It's because 'children just don't know how to entertain themselves anymore'. Even though we, as the adults, have not provided them with the same resources (i.e. space) to be able to entertain themselves outside. It is like conducting an experiment twice, but changing all the resources for the experiment, and telling the participants it is their fault when they get it wrong. If more children had access to an outdoor space at home, maybe they *would* go outside and kick a ball around.

Not having outdoor space at home also raises issues of security. If a child doesn't have a backyard to play in, they don't always have the option to go to a park on their own. As parents, of course, we can't be leaving our six-year-old at the park on their own (as much as we might like to, when little Taj has managed to push all of our buttons today). The truth is, we are more aware of the dangers in our neighbourhoods than we were 20 or 30 years ago. As urban populations have grown, so too has the scale, scope and complexity of the technological revolution that has influenced our behaviours and ways of living unlike anything humankind has experienced before (Schwab, 2015). The media is invited into our homes on a daily basis, communicating negative media stories that contribute to parents feeling too anxious to let their children engage in free play outdoors (James, 2007). Given they are increasingly concerned about safety (Veitch et al., 2006), parents restrict their children's external range even further, limiting access to nearby nature (Moore and Young, 1978). This means that children play predominately in managed urban-based play spaces (Skår and Krogh, 2009). These urban-based play spaces are often not gardens, but rather concrete environments (Moore et al., 2021). And, let's be real: kicking the ball around a concrete play space isn't going to increase children's connection to nature. While it is beneficial for their health and physical activity, in terms of nature connection we're back to square one.

All of this means more children are playing inside. So, what do children play inside? Well, sometimes they are playing with Lego or Beyblade tops or board games. On the very odd occasion they may be even reading – but don't get ahead of yourself, it's probably a graphic novel or a book about farts! In reality, technology has infiltrated the play space for most children. There's a rise of children on iPads or playing video games. Now, technology is not necessarily a bad thing. It can be very beneficial. However, the amount of time that children are spending on technology has increased since the change of the century. Technology may have contributed to the nature disconnect, as our children are quite simply spending less time in nature and more time looking at screens.

And you know why we let our children have more access to technology? Because we're tired. We live in a society where it's go, go, go. Quick, quick, quick.

Most families are now two-parent dual-working families. The cost of living has driven us to take time away from our children and input that into our working lives. I know so many parents who have gone back to working full-time because working part-time was just not enough to pay the bills – groceries are more expensive, interest rates on housing have increased, and Balthazar needs grommets surgery that isn't covered in our health insurance plan.

We need to work more because our houses are more expensive, and we can barely afford a house if only one person is working. And you know what? In addition to necessity, maybe we all *want* to work. Gender norms have changed, and many people across the gender spectrum want to work (and also want to look after their children). But the pressure of work and family makes it challenging to do both.

In Australia there is also a pervasive idea that we need to 'keep up with the Joneses'. It's exhausting. To me, the 'rat race' feels very similar to an actual race. And I'm not very good at races. I'm the mum who entered the 'Mother's Race' at my children's sports carnival and felt very confident and competitive on the start line, eyeing up the other parents, only to realise when the gun fired that I was not nearly as fast as I had imagined in my head. Trailing behind the other mothers, I had the feeling of life mirroring art (or vice versa). The metaphorical race of life had manifested into the physical realm. Afterwards, people kept tagging me in the viral video of the mother falling over in the parents' race, dress flung over her head and G-string on show to rows and rows of startled, scared and confused Year 1 to 3 kids. Surely I'm better than this? Maybe I, too, need more time for nature – trail running anyone?

The cycle of constant activity

Our lives are run in an eternal credit cycle. People want access to housing, because we need to put a roof over our family's head. We want access to good, reliable cars, because we've been pushed out of more centralised housing areas. We're no longer close to work due to the prices of the properties close to work, so we've moved further out to more 'affordable' areas. But, we also want to send our children to 'good schools', where they can thrive and grow. Which means that we sometimes end up driving further away to send our children to the 'good school'. We want the best for our children, so we encourage them into extracurricular activities to ensure that they have their sporting, cultural and artistic quench satisfied. The result is that we are up and down that main road several times a week – and there's less and less time for nature.

All of these wants, of course, stem from positive intentions. However, maybe we're actually disadvantaging our children. The idea of go, go, go, quick, quick, quick puts our children in a perpetual cycle of constant activity – and we can understand how that feels, because we ourselves are in a perpetual cycle of constant activity. In dual-parent families, we're both working. We have long days at work. We're trying to pay off our mortgage. We're trying to pay off our car debt. We're trying to afford groceries for our family. With the rising cost of living, we're trying to provide our children with positive opportunities, all of which is very noble. However, what it does create is less and less time for children to rest and relax; and, for that matter, parents to rest and relax. There's less time for everyone to have contact with nature.

And yes, I hear you saying: 'Oh, but it doesn't matter. I don't miss nature. I quite like my go, go, go, quick, quick, quick lifestyle. I like being constantly occupied and having fun and engaging. I love going to see my children do their sports or win their awards at school.' But it's important to reflect on this. We and our children may have lost our ability to connect with nature. What does that mean we are missing?

Look at the amount of extracurricular activities you and your children, or the children in your care, do per week. Is that restricting the time available to simply be in nature?

And while there are benefits, of course, of doing extracurricular activities, including the sport and cultural influences that your children could learn from in those activities, maybe we've started to miss the point.

Do the benefits that our children and ourselves get out of those extracurricular activities outweigh the benefits of simply having some nature connection?

Have we missed the point entirely? And, if we *have* missed the point entirely, more importantly, is it too late? And what do we do now? Where do we even begin?

Do we even know *how* to connect with nature? Why is it even important for us to connect with nature?

It feels overwhelming, doesn't it? Even though we are trying to everything right, sometimes it feels like we might be doing everything wrong. And we consider giving up.

Take a breath.

I want you to think back to your childhood. I know, hearing those stories of 'back in my day' can feel irritating. Our parents did it to us, and now we're going to do it to our children. How annoying and obnoxious of us. But you know what? As I get older, I think those stories of how things were for previous generations become more and more important (see how that might happen?). The past becomes more important because the world changes and evolves. And it changes and evolves so quickly that we don't even realise it, because we're in that go, go, go, quick, quick, quick mindset. In our highly urbanised societies where we're so physically enclosed and so emotionally engrossed in what we're doing during the day-to-day that we have forgotten the bigger picture – our connectivity to everything, and everything's connectivity to us. We have forgotten nature. We need to take the blinkers off and realise what's happening in the bigger, broader, greater world around us.

Those stories of 'back in my day' might actually be really important. So let's go back to those.

Returning to childhood

Let's think about our engagement with nature during our own childhoods. I'll give you an example: I grew up on a 100-tree mango farm in rural central Queensland. My siblings and I were quite frequently left to our own devices during the long summer holiday months. Now that I think back on it, it was probably a little bit inappropriate to leave three young children at home on their own on a property with snakes and other dangerous animals. But that's what happened to us back then. I wasn't all on my own. Being left to my own devices wasn't too bad with an older brother (two years older) and a younger sister (two years younger). And being on a huge mango property obviously was not a common experience, however, that was my experience.

Now, we were not farmers at all. My father, with his flamboyant pink shorts, is probably quite the opposite of what you'd imagine when you think of a farmer. A lot of the mangoes that were on those 100 trees just fell to the ground and rotted (again, not farmers). It was a work property, a house of circumstance tied to my father's job. Along with the mango trees we also had cows. Looking back, I have no idea what the cows were doing there. They were never taken to abattoirs or milked. They were just there. Present. Those cows must have been living their best lives, though, because all they did all day was slurp up mangoes and spit out the seeds. Those cows would be on a $20-a-day diet with all the mangoes they would eat! I enjoyed just being there, on the farm, and that's where my love of nature started.

It's hard because, as adults, we forget a lot of these formative experiences. Perhaps we don't think that we have the right to be experts or think that we know about connection with nature, because we're not researchers, we're not experts in this field. But everybody has had some experience with nature that they themselves are an expert on, because it's a lived experience. And I think we must harness that more in our role as teachers (and parents). You are an expert in nature connection simply because you have had connection with nature yourself (at one point or another). You have the right to be able to speak about your personal experiences and how they influenced your life as an educator, but also just as a person.

Think about those very important first-stage experiences you had in nature. Think about how you felt, what you smelt, what you were looking at, who you were with. The reality of those experiences may be co-constructed with the people that you were with, so talk to them (if you can). Do they have the same memory as you? Were their experiences of that time in nature and the nature connection that they felt the same as the memory and experiences that you had? Or different? Are you retelling the same story or are your experiences of the same memory slightly different, and why? There can be multiple truths to the same reality.

What I remember most about being on the mango farm is the long, dry grass and how it would whip your heels and your legs as you ran through it. It was a rush – a little painful but also liberating. I'll never forget that feeling, or the slight fear that I felt (because, you know, snakes). There was adrenaline in your body because there was a very real possibility of coming across something that could hurt you that you couldn't see! The wiggling of the high reeds made my heart beat faster. Most of the time it was only our pet cat Boots jumping out at us – the feline looking like a lion through the long grass of the savanna.

I also remember the daring competitions that I would have with my brother and sister. We had a huge bull-ant nest that was directly next to the big iron gate that we would open to our house. The gate separated the expansive farm, with the cows and the mango trees, from our smaller yard that we could enjoy closer to the house. The bull-ant nest was gigantic. Well, at least, it seemed huge to my eight-year-old self. We would dare each other to run over the nest. The first sibling would run over it, then the second sibling would run over it, and by the time it got to the third sibling, the ants would be starting to be stirred up a little and they would come out all agitated. Now, this probably wasn't very kind to nature, looking back, but I was a child and, to be honest, because I was left unsupervised, I didn't really know much better. I do regret that some ants were probably hurt in that process and it was not my intention.

What also happened, though, was that we were outside. These experiences connected me to nature. I started to understand that there is risk and reward in nature, and that nature is multifaceted – pain, excitement, trepidation, fear and love were all feelings I felt in nature. I learned that I could experience physical benefits from being outside and running around, but equally importantly, feelings of wellbeing and connection. I experienced success – if I crossed the bull-ant nest without being bitten, that was a marker of achievement (in the mind of my childhood self). I unfortunately experienced humans dominating nature, which is a very anthropocentric way of thinking I have come to realise as an adult. And sometimes nature dominated me. There was one instance where the bull ants bit my feet quite ferociously, which taught me a big lesson about treating nature with respect. After that I stopped running over the bull-ant nest.

As we grow older, many of us become separated from nature without even realising it. We move to bigger cities to attend university or gain access to employment. We buy houses in highly urbanised areas to be closer to work. And we slowly disconnect from nature in the process. We create that disconnect from nature for our children, too. They also live in the highly urbanised spaces with smaller backyards and little access to local parks. We may have *collectively* disconnected from nature. And even if we live close to nature, the way we live our lives might contribute to that disconnect, too. Eventually this can disintegrate into a form of apathy where we think, 'I don't care.' We might believe that nature doesn't fit into our day-to-day. We have too much work, our kids have too many extracurricular activities and there's simply too much going on to spend time in nature.

When I talk to people around me about nature connection, I hear retorts of disgruntlement or chortles of sarcasm. Some believe nature connection is only for hippie tree huggers – people who have all the time in the world to connect and meditate and be in nature. Sometimes the responses can be defensive, even aggressive. Because who has time for nature connection? Who even wants that? This creates nature deficiency, or even defiance.

The benefits of nature connection

There is much discussion celebrating the positive effects of nature interaction (Capaldi et al., 2014). This is particularly true for non-threatening nature, which fosters an increased concern for nature

(Depledge et al., 2019; Twohig-Bennett & Jones, 2018). As a result of the benefits that nature interaction can provide, it is imperative to prioritise opportunities for nature connection at the forefront of research agendas (Depledge et al., 2019; Watts et al., 2015). However, simply spending time in nature may be insufficient to obtaining the health and wellbeing benefits it offers (Louv, 2009). Research suggests that establishing a deep emotional connection with nature is necessary for benefiting from the positive outcomes, including positive influences on wellbeing and increased concern for nature, through frequent and meaningful interactions in natural spaces (Capaldi et al., 2014; Mackay & Schmitt, 2019; Pritchard et al., 2020).

A lack of exposure to nature in childhood can negatively influence environmental concern and may inhibit the development of pro-environmental behaviours as adults (Nisbet et al., 2009; Corraliza et al., 2012; Keniger et al., 2013; Larson & Miller, 2011; Lin et al., 2018). Early experiences in nature and a development of knowledge about the natural environment may be necessary but not entirely sufficient to support pro-conservation attitudes and behaviours as adults (Kals et al., 1999). Consequently, depriving children of early positive interactions with nature and subjecting them to potentially negative experiences of nature can predict reduced appreciation for nature and limit pro-environmental behaviours and attitudes as adults (Fuller et al., 2010; Keniger et al., 2013).

Children who have the opportunity for early, positive and regular interactions with nature tend to develop a deep awareness of the interdependent relationship between humans and the natural world (Giusti et al., 2014). These interactions with nature play an important role in promoting child wellbeing (Blanchet-Cohen & Elliot, 2011). Wellbeing, as outlined by the World Health Organization, encompasses aspects of physical, psychological, mental, emotional, economic, environmental, social and spiritual health (Musek & Polic, 2014; Meiselman, 2016). Consequently, as posited by Richardson et al. (2016), 'a connection to nature may provide people with resilience to meet the challenges of everyday life, while also facilitating exercise, social contact, and a sense of purpose'.

So essentially, if we have low connection with nature as children, we will have lower pro-environmentalist attitudes and behaviours as adults. We will have a lower desire to be in or defend nature, and eventually that will result in us not caring about what happens to the environment.

But rather than consistently focusing on the negatives, why don't we start focusing on the positives? Each of us can make more of a difference than we realise. It's that idea of 'tag, you're it'. Readers, I am tapping each one of you on the shoulder and asking you to have a go at solving this problem. And part of doing this is to focus on what's going right – on the possibilities we have to make a change with the children in our care, as educators and as parents. We need to hear that positive message from multiple perspectives – from teachers, from families, from children. Because what one perspective might see as 'truth', the other may not. But it is challenging to know what everyone is thinking (or doing) because, well, no one has ever studied it, until now. So, what are we doing well? In our highly urbanised environments, even in our very busy schedules where two parents are working and our children do huge amounts of extracurricular activity, what are we doing right? In what ways are we ensuring that we have nature connection, and what benefits are we getting out of it? The way that we perceive our sociocultural context will have a huge influence on that. So, we also have to reflect on who are we, what we believe, what is important to us and whether nature connection matters to us at all. If not, do we see what the consequences will be of a nature disconnection? What are all the possible solutions?

Nature, big and small

When I speak to people about nature connection, I ask, 'Where did all the gardens go?' When considering nature connection, people tend to automatically go to 'big nature'. They think of hiking in the mountains or going to the beach on the weekend and swimming in the sea. But what about small nature? What about immediate nature? What about nature in everyday life? Why aren't we thinking of those experiences? Big nature is often hard. Accessing big nature means taking the car and driving to the mountain so we can do that long hike. It means taking the kids to the beach so that we're able to go swimming. It means planning, it means resources, it often means a whole lot of time – time that we didn't have to begin with! There are a whole lot of different parameters needed to make big nature happen. That's difficult. That's challenging. Personally, I can't do big nature. Not right now and not all the time. Especially not whenever I want quick and easy nature access.

Let's change our concept of nature connection and think about nature in our immediate environment. Where do our kids experience nature the most? Where do they regularly have access to nature?

Our children spend more time in formalised schooling than not. So it makes sense to consider how we might get more nature connection into formalised schooling. Now, I can hear you, all you teachers. Please remember, I'm a teacher myself, so I agree with you. Let's not place more pressure on teachers. Teachers already have an enormous amount of responsibility along with ever-increasing administration and red tape and challenges that have evolved in the last ten years. So let's not place more pressure on teachers.

But I'm not talking about integrating nature into education as a very formalised construct. Let's think about this very simplistically and document where nature already is within the educational environment. The school you work in might have large, expansive sporting spaces such as ovals, or a bush tucker garden, or a fairy garden. It might have virtual nature in terms of videos of natural spaces and photographs of nature in and around the school. All nature is important.

Of course, when I think of nature and education my mind goes straight to school gardens. School gardens have received increased attention over the last decade or so (Whitehead, 2018). Within the framework of our deteriorating sociality and relationship with nature, researchers have directed efforts towards nature spaces to re-examine the thoughts and behaviours of humanity and the various, and potentially intersecting, benefits children gain from nature spaces (Okely et al., 2021). However, while there has been an increase in research on the benefits of gardens for children, these are predominately theoretical (Ohly et al., 2016). Research has identified the positive impacts of school gardens for children (Chawla et al., 2014; Block et al., 2012; Ahmed et al., 2011; Alexander et al., 1995; Bowker & Tearle, 2007; Cutter-Mackenzie, 2009; Henryks, 2011; Viola, 2006). However, most of the emerging evidence on school gardens is quantitative and has a strong focus on improving children's willingness, preferences for consumption, and knowledge of fruit and vegetables (Ohly et al., 2016) and the improved health and nutrition benefits for children (Burt et al., 2017; Gatto et al., 2017). Wolsey and Lapp (2014) suggest that the complex systems of school gardens are often reduced to simplistic approaches that do not effectively characterise how the various elements in the system are interrelated.

There are minimal research studies that explore school gardens from a more holistic, strengths-based approach. It is possible that school gardens are being used in ways that have not been previously understood or explored by the literature. It's also possible that the discourses articulated around school garden research reflect the political and social values of the surrounding society, rendering school gardens unwelcoming or inaccessible spaces for certain groups of students (Oulton & Jagger, 2023). The impact of colonisation on agricultural practices has further complicated this issue, as traditional Aboriginal or Torres Strait Islander agricultural methods have often been marginalised or replaced, potentially influencing the design and inclusivity of school gardens. This book will help you as a teacher to explore the nuanced perceptions, experiences and meaning of school gardens through an in-depth reflective process and a focus on the varied and multifaceted benefits of school gardens.

Of course, school gardens received plenty of attention during the Covid-19 pandemic when there was an immediate and necessary focus on outdoor spaces at school. The World Health Organization encouraged teachers to move classes outside as much as possible to increase social distancing and curb the spread of the virus (Education in Emergencies UNICEF, 2020). Post-Covid, more and more schools are creating school garden spaces. The curriculum has changed to factor in school gardens and the environment, but what if teachers and students aren't using school gardens in that way? What if we are using school gardens as a very informal space? What if we let children tell *us* how they want to connect with school gardens rather than us implementing a top-down, adult-to-child approach to integrating school gardens, to curriculum and discourses? School gardens are a potential solution and the power may be in the people and place… if we just listen to the narratives.

Journal entry one

What is our school garden?

Writing your school garden story is a big part of 'setting the scene' for the current interactions, uses and benefits of the garden that we will explore in later chapters. As each school garden has different sociocultural influences that shape the school garden story, it is important that you capture your context clearly in this first journal entry. Let's get documenting! Feel free to add any photos (either historical or present-day) that you think will help describe your school garden context.

- When was our school garden established? By whom?
- What motivated the beginning of our school garden?
- What sort of community is our school garden located in?
- How has the community evolved over time?
- How has the school garden evolved over time?

If you don't currently have a school garden (but would like to establish one), think about the following questions:

- What are our primary motivations for starting a school garden?
- Who will be involved in the planning and establishment of the school garden?
- What sort of community is our school located in, and how might the garden serve this community?
- What resources and support are available within our community for starting a school garden?
- How can we design the school garden to be inclusive and welcoming for all students?
- What are our short-term and long-term goals for the school garden?

- How can we integrate the school garden into our existing curriculum and school activities?
- What steps will we take to ensure the sustainability and maintenance of the school garden?
- How will we measure the success and impact of the school garden on our students and community?

When you consider the community, here are some sub-questions to guide you:

- What are the demographic characteristics of our community (for example, age, ethnicity, socioeconomic status)?
- What are the predominant cultural and social values in our community?
- What local resources (for example, businesses, organisations, skilled individuals) can support our school garden project?
- How do community members typically engage with outdoor spaces and gardening activities?
- Are there any existing community gardens or similar projects in the area that we can collaborate with or learn from?
- What are the main environmental conditions in our community (for example, climate, soil quality, available space)?
- What challenges might our community face that could impact the success of a school garden (for example, vandalism, lack of interest, funding)?
- How can we involve community members in the planning, creation and maintenance of the school garden?
- What potential partnerships with local groups or organisations can be formed to support the school garden?
- What are the specific needs and interests of our community that the school garden could address or fulfil?

ACTION PLAN

Evaluate the current usage and potential of the school garden

Begin by assessing how your school garden is currently used. Is it incorporated into the curriculum? Does it remain an underutilised space? Identify potential areas for informal use and consider how the garden can be more effectively integrated into everyday school activities.

Informal use can include designing the garden with benches and tables so that small groups of students are able to eat their lunch in the school garden. There might also be some raised beds that are there for experimental play. Irrigation systems can be defined through experimentation (seeing where water flows and collects) before any plants are planted. Even the layering of the garden might be an experiment, with paper potentially used on some beds (to keep weeds from growing) in comparison to beds that do not have newspaper in their layering. Student-directed experimentation and peer learning is a very positive aspect of school gardens that are used informally (potentially in addition to formally).

Engage students in the planning process

Shift from a top-down approach to a more inclusive method by involving students in the planning and decision-making process. Hold class discussions, surveys or focus groups to gather their ideas on how they would like to use the garden. This approach empowers students and ensures that the garden meets their interests and needs.

Encourage informal use of the garden

Promote the garden as a space for informal activities rather than just structured lessons. Allow students to use the garden during breaks, after school or as a place for quiet reflection. This can include activities such as reading, drawing or simply enjoying the outdoors.

Develop a flexible curriculum integration plan

Create a flexible plan that incorporates the garden into various subjects without making it feel like a forced addition. Encourage teachers to use the garden for spontaneous lessons that connect with their curriculum organically. For example, a science teacher might use the garden to teach about plant biology, while an art teacher might use it for drawing classes.

Document the history and evolution of the school garden to create a narrative

In addition to your journal entry work, engage staff, students and community members to build a comprehensive history of your garden. A garden's power lies in the narratives of the people who use it. Collect stories and experiences from students, teachers and community members. This can be done through interviews, journal entries or creative projects. These narratives will help to understand the different ways the garden is valued and utilised.

Promote ongoing reflection and documentation

Encourage students and teachers to keep journals documenting their experiences and interactions with the garden. This ongoing reflection helps to continually assess the garden's impact and how it can be improved. Use these journals to identify patterns, successes and areas needing attention.

Host regular community events

Organise events that bring the school community together in the garden. This can include garden work days, educational workshops or social gatherings. These events help to foster a sense of ownership and investment in the garden.

Adapt and evolve based on feedback

Regularly review the feedback and reflections collected from students, teachers and community members. Use this information to adapt and evolve the garden's usage to better meet the needs and desires of the school community. Be flexible and open to change, ensuring that the garden remains a dynamic and responsive space.

Celebrate and share successes

Highlight and celebrate the successes and positive impacts of the garden on the school community. Share these stories in school newsletters, on social media or through school assemblies. Recognising these achievements helps to maintain enthusiasm and support for the garden.

TWO

BILLY THE KID

WHY ARE SCHOOL GARDENS IMPORTANT?

It's no secret that our go, go, go, quick, quick, quick lifestyles and increased indoor play are making us unhealthy. We are tired. We are stressed. We are apathetic. We are fat. And our children are, too. It's challenging, because we don't want to be those things. We want to be fit, healthy and happy, but because of our increasing disconnect from nature, it is almost like we've forgotten how to be. We can find ourselves in that death spiral of helplessness. But this can all change by focusing on the positives. We haven't got it *all* wrong. In fact, we have some of it very, very right! Hoorah! We understand that school gardens have many benefits for students (West, 2022) and, in Australia, gardening has experienced a resurgence since the late nineteenth century (Whitehead, 2018).

There is a growing body of research and public discourse advocating for the benefits of gardening in relation to personal, social and community health (Kingsley et al., 2019). But what are the benefits of school gardens? Who is reaping those benefits? And what do those benefits look like in reality? Are we inadvertently perpetuating societal norms and further marginalising certain groups of students through our school garden experiences?

In the introduction to this book I told you about Billy, the student who responded to my question about where tomatoes come from with 'from the supermarket'. This moment was a turning point for me. I saw the disconnect between children and the source of their food, and this fuelled my commitment to researching and promoting school gardens.

In truth, Billy reminded me of myself as a child – curious, intelligent yet a bit awkward and uncertain. I was no stranger to expansive spaces as a kid, but the hustle and bustle of school playgrounds often felt overwhelming. It was in the garden where I found a place to reflect, potter and just 'be'.

For me, the memory of the textures of a plant I brought into our school garden when I was in Year 1 is vivid. In Toowoomba, where I attended school at the time, the cold weather meant the plant had a soft and furry exterior that I loved rubbing between my fingers at lunchtime. Sharing the joy of this texture with my friends made me proud and helped me connect with my peers. As an adult, I still rub lavender flowers over my hand as I walk to our little community library, being careful not to damage them, and breathe in their fragrant smells. This simple act brings me immense joy and reminds me of the interconnectedness of the world around me. It is a testament to how deeply we are all connected to nature and each other.

In this chapter, we celebrate school gardens and their benefits for physical activity, health, wellbeing and experiential learning, and their positive social and academic impact. We also explore whether the benefits of school garden experiences extend to *all* students or if there are some we are inadvertently excluding (Taylor et al., 2021).

Billy wants to eat well and be physically active

What I found when I began researching school gardens is that most school garden interventions aim to increase fruit and vegetable consumption in children (Kararo et al., 2016). School gardens are being used as our 'fix it' tool to boost nutritional knowledge and consumption to address childhood obesity (Landry et al., 2021). And it's no wonder, really. Billy loves pizza. I mean, pizza is so accessible for Billy. It's on his tuckshop menu (along with meat pies, hamburgers and hot dogs); it is sold at his local surf club where he goes for dinner with his family (along with fish and chips, and chicken nuggets and chips); it's at home, because his parents are too tired to cook after their full-time work days, and cheap Tuesday means it's only $5 for a whole pizza, so why not?

Billy doesn't know that pizza isn't really what his body needs – he demonstrated that in his response about where tomatoes came from. And it's not Billy's fault. But all is not lost. School gardens could be a viable solution to increasing children's nutritional knowledge and physical activity. Children who grow their own food are more likely to eat fruits and vegetables (Dyment & Bell, 2008). And school gardens expose children to new foods (West, 2022). Wouldn't it be great if Billy knew where tomatoes came from, but also knew about how other less traditional fruits and vegetables grow? He would know that pineapples reign on their throne, that asparagus stand up and dance in the sunshine, and that passionfruit creep their way along the garden on an entanglement of vines.

Increased physical activity and healthy eating form the reasoning for many school garden interventions (Van Dijk-Wesselius et al., 2020). Children who are involved in school gardens demonstrate higher levels of nutritional knowledge (Koch et al., 2006). The British Psychological Society conducted research on students' attitudes about eating fruit and vegetables before and after participating in a 12-week program to create a school garden (Christian et al., 2014). Before participation in the school garden program, students had difficulty distinguishing healthy and unhealthy food choices.

Results demonstrated that after the school garden program, students increased their fruit and vegetable consumption by 26 per cent. A similar result was presented by Jones et al. (2012) via research on the UK's Food for Life (FFL) program. The results showed that students had more holistic approaches to food, and the consumption of organic food doubled after exposure to the FFL program.

School gardens not only increase nutritional knowledge, but they can increase physical activity, too. Imagine Billy enjoying all the colours, textures and sounds as he moves around the school garden. Fjørtoft and Sageie (2000) posited that green landscaping can encourage students to engage in a diverse array of outdoor activities. Student participation in school-based green spaces appeared to improve overall student health and physical condition, evident in lower absence rates for illness than previously reported. School gardens have also been found to increase incidental walking for students (Warshaw & Bolderman, 2008). You can see Billy now – jumping from log to log, bending to smell the low-lying flowers, reaching up high to pick apples or oranges, or running around the perimeter of the garden to observe the passionfruit vines. But that's not all that Billy needs out of his school garden experience...

Billy needs a friend

Billy doesn't have many friends. At home, his parents are often on their technology devices – because the work-from-home culture has invited itself further into their family space, and because they are so exhausted from their long working hours that they use their devices to 'escape'. Billy often wonders what his parents want to escape from – he's right there. But sadly, Billy's parents don't talk to him much anymore. In fact, there aren't any noises in the house. His parents are death scrolling, caught in the endless loop of mindless down, down, down – a bit like Alice falling in the hole after the rabbit. Billy's siblings have noise-cancelling headphones and are on their tablets. So, Billy is all alone, and he feels it – he feels it to his core. He's five. And he really needs a friend.

The school garden could be a lifeline for Billy. Gardens are spaces for people to gather, share and act together (Shepard, 2009). Children gain enjoyment from interacting with their peers in school gardens; the friendship, or even side-by-side interaction, that occurs in the school garden environment fosters a sense of belonging with peers, promoting overall child wellbeing (Chawla et al., 2014). The building of social relationships with peers in school gardens is important as these relationships may benefit the students for their entire life journey (Lucke et al., 2019). School gardens support child social development through relationship-building, which has a lifelong impact (Block et al., 2012). This social development is fostered in school gardens as the space provides students with an ability to play with other children. Recreational spaces in schools are designed to foster students' choices of play space through their diverse modalities (Papadopoulou et al., 2020). The green space of a school garden proposes further variety for child stimulation and may be a favourable environment for the development of 21st-century skills (Jana, 2018). Through the school garden, Billy may have the opportunity to interact with children (and adults) that he wouldn't otherwise have any contact with – this may be children from other grades, or teachers of different specialist areas from whom he can learn new skills or simply converse.

Billy is actively connection-seeking. He wants friends. He wants someone to talk to – even more than that, he *needs* someone to talk to, to calm the emptiness he feels inside, day in and day out. He doesn't understand it – he just knows that is doesn't feel good. And Billy wants to feel good. He *deserves* to feel good. Maybe connection will help him feel good. And connection happens in the school garden.

Billy likes Ms Rossi

Ms Rossi is, after all, very likeable. She can be equally loud and exuberant, waving her hands around with passion while telling a story about how the sunflowers grow; and calm and caring, nurturing Billy and chatting to him while they simply sit in the sun. Billy wonders why Ms Rossi is so nice to him. Or why she is even in the garden at all? He doesn't think she is paid for it. (She's not – she volunteers to supervise the garden on her lunchbreak, so that children like Billy can enjoy the garden.) Ms Rossi loves the garden. Like Billy, she enjoys the opportunity to connect with people (other staff and students) who she may not usually have contact with in her day-to-day classroom teaching. She appreciates the school garden as a meeting place.

School gardens can be gathering spaces that foster diversity. A study by Cutter-Mackenzie (2009) produced evidence from a multi-cultural program where students from a diverse range of cultural backgrounds interacted in a school garden. In this research, the school garden acted as a space for meeting, developing relationships and sharing information through exposure to students from other cultures (Cutter-Mackenzie, 2009).

Ms Rossi sometimes talks to Billy about tomatoes, filling the gaps in his knowledge. She does this from a sociocultural perspective. You see, Ms Rossi is an immigrant. She migrated to Australia five years ago to follow her partner who was transferred with his company. But Ms Rossi sometimes misses Italy, and speaking Italian. She tells Billy about the big family celebrations her relatives would have together, picking the tomatoes from her grandmother's garden and coming together with all of her aunts, uncles and cousins to cook the fruit in their grandmother's kitchen. She remembers her hands smelling of tomato stems and peeling the skin off the hot boiled flesh, which she always felt was a bit of a daredevil task. She misses it.

Ms Rossi may not have realised it, as adults seldom do, but she needs connection, too. As she finishes up talking to Billy about the family tomato celebration, she realises that she has a tear in her eye – a very stubborn tear that does not fall down her face. It holds, resilient. Billy sees it and silently wraps his arms around her in a side-on hug. It's awkward. More of a lean than a hug, really, but both feel better after their interaction in the school garden. Each bringing the other something they were seeking, even if they didn't know that they were seeking it.

Billy would like to do well at school

Maybe that would make his parents proud, and then they would talk to him – congratulate him, even. School gardens have been evidenced to support student performance (Akerlof et al., 2013). Passy, Morris and Reed (2010) researched the influence of school gardening on students' behaviour and learning. Their qualitative study involved ten schools and the results demonstrated that school gardens have a positive social and emotional effect on students. Student participation in school gardens enabled students to broaden their knowledge and capabilities. Students learned life skills and could identify the natural progression and changing of the seasons, food harvesting and preparation through the school garden program. Students developed leadership skills, responsibility and self-esteem, supporting their growth as active and capable citizens. The perceptions and attitudes towards the school and education prospered both within the student cohort and the wider community.

Billy gets distracted in the classroom. It's so beige. He notices the beige as he spends a good part of the day staring at the beige walls. The walls are definitely beige. However, when Billy is outside, it's a different story. It's bright, and flexible, and dynamic. School gardens can benefit children who do not necessarily excel in academic settings, including children with learning or behavioural challenges. These children are able to explore their abilities and successes in a different and less formal way through interactions with the school garden (Ohly et al., 2016). Taylor, Kuo and Sullivan (2001) explored the correlation between nature and gardening on one hand and learning on the other. The participants were students with attention deficit disorder (ADD). The results demonstrated that exposure to the green spaces within the school lessened the intensity of ADD symptoms, compared with non-green spaces. Regular daily opportunities to connect with gardens appeared to reduce the symptoms of ADD for these specific students. Billy wants to concentrate. He makes an active choice to seek out the garden at playtime to see if that will help.

What Billy loves the most is that other people are proud of him. Ms Rossi overheard an interaction with Billy the other day. Maya said, 'I like your sunflower seeds, Billy.' Billy had a wry smile. He was so proud. Success is supported by peer recognition through achievement and pride that children experience from their school gardens. The school garden provides space for children to gain confidence and self-esteem and provides the opportunity to demonstrate ownership and responsibility (Chiumento et al., 2018). These feelings contribute to a sense of achievement and pride from caring for the plants and watching them grow. A study by Maller (2005) compared the effects on children's psychological health from experiential learning and activities in a school garden compared with other green spaces within schools. The results demonstrated that while all activities in nature were beneficial to student psychological health and self-confidence, school garden activities encouraged communication, cooperation and collaboration which supported students working towards a common goal. School gardens provide students with an opportunity to be together, that this is satisfying for students. School gardens, compared with other green spaces, resulted in stronger peer relationships and attitudes towards school (Waliczek et al., 2001). Children are able to come together in different ways in school gardens that they aren't able to in other school environments.

Billy appreciates the school garden for the experiential learning opportunities and knowledge development. The school garden provides an environment in which students are able to acquire the ability to construct knowledge on their own through their own experiential learning. Students are able to develop knowledge through their active involvement in tangible situations presented in the school garden. This 'learning by doing' is a key component of educational theory as outlined by Dewey and helps students to understand the world through interactions and actions

(Garitsis, 2016). Through experiential learning, children have direct and hands-on experiences to construct new knowledge, skills and values (Bowker & Tearle, 2007). School gardens can, therefore, support the development of the 21st-century skills of creativity, curiosity, communication, collaboration, critical thinking, grit, leadership and adaptability (Jana, 2018). These skills are developed through the real-life experiences and hands-on techniques presented within the school garden (Eames-Sheavly, 1994; Skelly & Zajicek, 1998; Lineberger & Zajicek, 2000; Robinson & Zajicek, 2005). This more holistic approach to school garden research, focused on how people are interacting with school gardens as a whole, may unveil the learning of particular life skills for specific sets of students not previously represented in school garden research. Billy is thriving, appreciating the garden for the many benefits it provides, but what about other children? Are all children able to benefit from school garden experiences? Or is the celebration that school gardens are beneficial for *all* students potentially overshadowing that they may be unwelcoming or inaccessible for certain groups of students?

Is everyone a Billy?

School gardens are valuable green spaces within educational settings and are celebrated for positively influencing opportunities for outdoor learning, social and emotional development and wellbeing, child growth, health and development (Dring et al., 2020). School gardens have been hailed as spaces that promote experiential learning, promoting environmental and sustainability goals and practices, and reinforcing a STEM curriculum in an outdoor 'real-world' setting (Okiror et al., 2011; Graves et al., 2016). As a result of the research highlighting the positive benefits of school gardens, there is a dominant discourse that posits that school gardens are positive spaces for all students (Blair, 2009).

Recently, however, some are questioning whether school gardens are truly beneficial spaces for all students (Taylor et al., 2021). Certain groups of students may not feel that school gardens are welcoming or accessible. This may reflect values embedded into the societal discourse, potentially further marginalising some students (Andersson & Borg, 2023). Colonialist values, which are still very prevalent in Australian society, may inadvertently influence school garden research (Oulton & Jagger, 2023). Colonialist views are perpetuated through the traditionally British agricultural practices that are integrated into the Australian educational systems (Lochner, 2019). These perspectives may limit certain gardens, such as bush tucker gardens, from being part of the primary school garden discourse. This, of course, may result in a limited representation of certain groups of students, such as Aboriginal and Torres Strait Islander students, whose agricultural traditions may not conform to the dominant discourse of school gardens. A potentially colonialist discourse of school gardens may prevent certain groups from feeling welcome or represented in the garden (Coomber, 2022).

School gardens may further perpetuate divisions based on class or ethnicity, too (Oulton & Jagger, 2023). Students who do not have gardens at home due to living in urban settings or public housing may feel that their lack of interaction with garden environments contributes to their discomfort in school garden settings (Rees & Melix, 2019). Students who live in highly urbanised public housing settings are often from lower socioeconomic families; unease in school garden contexts may deepen the divide between them and their peers, or further reinforce societal discourses of assimilation (Oulton & Jagger, 2023).

Societal values can also be perpetuated through school garden discourses in relation to gender roles. Traditional gender roles can be highlighted or even encouraged in school garden contexts, with boys being seen as the physical and active participants and the girls being seen as passive caretakers or observers (Lupinacci et al., 2022). As Taylor et al. (2021) posit, the tools that are used and the division of tasks can further contribute to gender biases and may contribute to women feeling unwelcome or unequal within the school garden.

School gardens should be welcoming and accessible environments for all students. Some school garden spaces may be overwhelming spaces that negatively impact student concentration (Petersson, 2022). School gardens with excessive stimuli may create an environment that is inaccessible to students with specific sensory needs. All students' sensory needs should be considered when planning school garden design and activities.

The current school garden discourses seem to highlight the benefits for 'normal' children. What is left out of the equation is the ability for certain groups of children to both access and feel welcomed in school garden spaces (Cohen & Jimenez, 2008). It is therefore very important to explore how meaning-making is constructed in the discourses on school gardens. School gardens may be inadvertently marginalising certain groups of students, which means that they are not beneficial for all students as previously celebrated by dominant school garden discourses in research.

Journal entry two

Why is our school garden important?

Reflecting on why your school garden is important is a big part of giving your school garden meaning. How is meaning being made in your school garden, and by whom? The dominant discourses of society, but also within the school, will influence how meaning-making occurs in the school garden and thus, the benefits for some or all students. Here are some questions to consider:

- Who is using our school garden?
- Is the use formal or informal?
- Who is benefiting from our school garden?
- Are there certain groups of students who are *not* benefiting from our school garden, or who may feel unwelcome or unrepresented?
- What is our school garden's role in promoting physical activity, mental health, social interaction and academic learning?
- How does the garden contribute to the overall wellbeing of students and the wider school community?

ACTION PLAN

Assess who is using the garden

Identify who is currently using the garden, and how. Are the activities primarily formal, such as structured classes, or informal, such as free play during breaks? Take note of which students are most engaged with the garden, and during which times of the day or week the garden is most utilised.

Evaluate the benefits being gained

Consider who is benefiting from the garden, and how. Are certain groups of students, such as specific age groups or classes, gaining more from the garden than others? Reflect on how the garden activities support their physical, emotional and social development.

Identify groups not benefiting

Look for groups of students who might not be benefiting from the garden. Are there certain demographics, such as students with special needs, older students or those from different cultural backgrounds, who are less engaged? Consider why these groups might not be using or benefiting from the garden as much.

Understand how meaning is being made

Reflect on how meaning is being made in the garden and by whom. Consider the dominant discourses within the school and society that influence how the garden is perceived and used. Are there cultural or social factors that shape the way different groups of students interact with the garden?

Adapt activities to be more inclusive

Based on your reflections, adapt garden activities to be more inclusive. Create programs that cater to the needs and interests of under-represented groups. This might include sensory activities for special needs students, cultural planting projects for diverse groups or leadership roles for older students.

Promote informal and flexible use

Encourage informal and flexible use of the garden. Allow students the freedom to explore and use the garden outside of structured class times. Promote the garden as a space for play, relaxation and social interaction, helping to integrate it more fully into daily school life.

Create a supportive environment

Foster a supportive environment where students feel safe and encouraged to use the garden. Address any barriers to participation, such as safety concerns or lack of resources, to ensure all students can benefit from the garden.

THREE

THE VENUS FLYTRAP

MEANING-MAKING IN THE SCHOOL GARDEN

I once went to a pottery class – mostly because my neighbour encouraged me to, she had wine and I tend to be a 'yes' person. But I hate pottery. I dislike any arts or crafts, to be honest, which I guess is slightly at odds with being a teacher – particularly one who enjoys the early years – but there you have it! The truth is, I wasn't going to the pottery class for the art. I was going to hang out with my friend. The making was just a means to connect with other people.

The art studio was in the front room of the teacher's house. It was an old home, with wooden single-pane windows. In my analytical brain, I kept thinking how easy this place would be to break into, and how cold it must get in winter. As I was looking around and assessing for break-in-ability, scanning with my integrated eye lasers, I noticed the eclectic nature of the room. There were things everywhere: pieces of broken pottery on the floor, splotches of paint on the table, scars of a painting frenzy gone wrong. And I immediately liked the character of the person moving out of the shadows of the corner of the room towards me. Her dark wavy hair was quite literally thrown up into a bun. She was very small and was wearing an apron. *I can't remember the last time I saw someone wearing an apron*, I thought.

Then my pondering was interrupted by the thud of a ball of clay hitting the paint massacre of a table. Without thinking, I let out a large sigh. I don't actually like the texture of clay. I'm a bit texture-averse at times. My friend picked up on my sigh and smiled. She knows I am a perfect mix of uncomfortable and stubborn, and therefore too damn determined not to make this the best piece of pottery I possibly could, just to prove myself, while at the same time hating touching the clay. This is both a strength and a weakness, and I'm very aware of it.

The teacher said, 'Make whatever you like.' The lack of direction was concerning for me, but I rallied. *Okay, you got this*, I said to myself. A Venus flytrap, of all things, was what came to mind, and I started 'creating'. (Eww.)

Of course, as often happens when you meet new people, the teacher asked me about myself. I told her of my interest in school garden research and our talk quickly escalated into enthusiasm. I shared that while learning in outdoor environments can provide enrichment for children and strengthen educational practice, they can be largely inaccessible spaces for teachers and students (Goodall, 2016). Most literature about outdoor learning is concerned with activities that are outside the school premises (Van Dijk-Wesselius et al., 2020). Field trips, forest school and external nature programs all provide opportunities for children to connect with nature (Sahrakhiz et al., 2018); however, while these outdoor activities are beneficial to children, teachers are often faced with barriers that hinder their ability to facilitate and improve children's access to nature environments due to time, resources and curriculum (Fischer, 2018; Edwards-Jones et al., 2018). This results in time in nature being put into the 'too hard basket'.

Too hard. Can't do it. Won't do it. No, thank you.

But what about inside the school footprint?

I went on to tell the pottery teacher that one of the most interesting school gardening experiences I have had was with only a few vines along a wall as a vertical garden. It's almost as if the vines were 'bouldering' – fearless wall climbers, unharnessed, unhinged and completely free. This particular school was a very urban school, four walls, almost all bitumen, almost zero green space. However, even in that highly urbanised school, there was a creative way of having some nature connection. The students in this school had vines all around the walls of their recreational space. The vines were essentially the only green that there was in the whole school – and it was a considerably big school in terms of student population and physical footprint within the centre of a highly dense and urbanised community.

The vines on these walls were grape vines, and the students witnessed grapes growing from small buds. Once the fruit was ready to be picked, two volunteers from the community were invited into the school grounds to manage the grape picking and crushing. The volunteers really looked the part: they were small and wore patchwork waistcoats. Their hands were weathered, and they both had deep lines of black around their yellowed fingernails from a lifetime of manual labour. Their faces were wrinkled and spotted, but equally animated and joyous. Each was so passionate and ready to share their knowledge and love of the grape picking and crushing process with the children.

I had my prep students all ready to go – we were armed and adventurous! We hadn't formally learnt about plant cycles or the harvesting process. This was an all-organic experience – not curriculum-driven, not from a textbook, not mandated by the 'higher-ups'. Not even very well-planned, if I'm honest. We were just doing it because of our love of the garden. And why not? It was a unique experience and so worthy to anchor into that intergenerational knowledge.

The children, driven by their natural curiosity, began to ask questions of the strangers – what was the garden like when you were at this school? How is it different today? What do you think happened over that time? What are your suggestions for improvement? Would you simply like to come by and hang out in the garden more often? Please? Pretty please? Pinky promise?

I gave the prep children responsibility for using secateurs to cut the grapes off the vine, and then put those grapes into a bucket and use their bare feet to crush them. Now, I know what you're thinking. I know your brain is immediately going to OHS guidelines and administrative requirements. But before you do, let me reassure you that this happened overseas, in France more precisely, where the OHS requirements are vastly different and probably slightly (*beaucoup*) more lenient than in Australia. I also know that in Australia we have a lot of red tape, potentially too much red tape, which is one of the reasons a lot of teachers don't encourage school garden experiences in their teaching – simply because it's just too hard, too time-consuming to set up, too emotionally and mentally exhausting. *Sigh* I'm tired even contemplating a garden experience.

But, back to the Frenchies – in this school the children cut the grapes off the vine with sharp secateurs. I would love to say that they then carefully placed the grapes in a bucket, taking great care to preserve the fine skin and firmness of the grapes, but that would be a lie. The kids took great joy in flinging the grapes over the sides of the great big wooden barrel, to shouts of 'Hoorah!', giggling and cheering. It was almost like the grape Olympics.

Then, the children all took off their shoes, washed their feet and crushed all the grapes. They pounded, jumped on, squashed, smooshed and squeezed those grapes. The joy on their faces! The laughter! The colours! The excitement! All these feelings were because of an experience that involved not only the school garden, but one another. You see, they had a chance to work together, be happy together, talk together, laugh together and love together.

In an instant, they could see that juice was coming out of the tap at the bottom of the barrel. What a triumph! We did it!

The community volunteers were a big part of the success of that moment. Again, it wasn't a 'project' or 'initiative'. It wasn't particularly organised or manufactured – it was simply a moment in time. This simple act of 'being in a moment in time' is an important way of making meaning of school garden experiences (Yanow, 2006).

During this 'moment in time', the volunteers, both of whom had attended the historical school themselves, were talking about the cultural aspect of the grapes and what it meant for a community to harvest the grapes and crush them together, and celebrate the grape picking once a year. It was really interesting for the students to be able to have that physical connection to nature through the crushing of the grapes by their feet, but also the cultural aspect of feeling part of something much bigger than themselves in the school garden. It allowed them to see their place within a community. The children created meaning from this experience. Their meaning was created from their 'being', their 'doing' and their 'belonging' (Hammel, 2004). These would drive them towards their own 'becoming', as the volunteers provided a window through time to part of a future that awaited them as contributing members of their community.

The four dimensions of meaning

Hammel (2004) distinguishes four dimensions of meaning: themes that people use to discuss their realities. These are *doing, being, belonging* and *becoming*. Hammel's four dimensions of meaning focus on the humanistic aspect of meaning-making (Musich et al., 2018). The performance of tasks, connections and acquisition of skills within a space generate meaning, through which a space is transformed into a place (Rowles, 2008).

The first dimension of Hammel's framework is the aspect of *doing*. Doing is the dimension of meaning that emphasises an active engagement and the behaviours associated with an activity within an environment. In the context of school gardens, meaning could be derived from active participation – including planting, watering, weeding or educating (Ong et al., 2019). Doing is one of the core dimensions of meaning celebrated in research that explores the meaning attributed to community gardens. The studies by Ong et al. (2019) and Lucke et al. (2019) both emphasised doing as the most significant dimension of meaning within community gardens. Physical actions and a sense of agency and accomplishment derived from one's personal contributions to the garden are all important aspects of doing as a dimension of meaning.

The second dimension of Hammel's framework is the element of *being*. Being is a concentrated focus on oneself, one's identity and the individual meaning that people associate with engagement with school gardens. Different stakeholders within school gardens may attribute meaning in diverse ways through their perspective of being as a dimension of meaning. For example, teachers may assume a role as a nurturer, leader or environmental activist by being in the school garden – but these roles are largely undocumented in a formal sense, as research has not been previously conducted in this area. Teachers' roles, values and connection with others and nature may influence the nuanced meanings that they attribute to the school garden space, but it is unclear if this occurs or how these roles manifest in practice. The experiences of children in the garden can shape their sense of self, providing them with opportunities to explore, learn and develop a personal connection with nature.

Belonging is the third dimension of Hammel's four dimensions of meaning. The belonging aspect focuses on the interpersonal relationships and interactions that occur within school gardens. Teachers may attribute meaning to the school garden through the collaborative experiences with children, colleagues and community members within this space. The community garden research by Connelly et al. (2012) and Ong et al. (2019) emphasised the importance of belonging within community gardens and how this formed one of the integral elements that gave people a sense of meaning. Teachers' interactions and the feeling of belonging that they experience in these spaces may influence the significance and meaning they attach to school gardens. However, Taylor et al. (2021) suggest that school gardens may not be accessible or welcoming spaces for all, which may negatively impact the dimension of belonging as a key aspect of meaning-making in school gardens. The sense of belonging that children feel through interactions with their peers, parents, teachers and community members within the school garden can foster a supportive and inclusive environment.

Hammel's final dimension of meaning, *becoming*, focuses on personal transformation and growth . Teachers may learn new skills, have a shift in values or attitudes, or undergo personal growth that contributes to their overall feeling of becoming – a move towards growth and development. Ong et al. (2019) found that becoming, through skills development and personal growth, was a way in which people attributed meaning to community gardens. Teachers may attribute meaning to the school garden through their own subjective experiences of becoming or through the experiences of becoming that they witness in children and families. Alternatively, in contrast to the meaning attributed to community gardens, becoming may not feature as an aspect of meaning in school gardens at all.

Now that we understand the framework for meaning, it is clear that my prep children developed a connection to the community via the volunteers who had spoken about their experiences. This enabled them to see the cultural identity of their community. This is what Hammel (2004) is referring to through the dimension of belonging – that every school garden stakeholder (teachers, students, parents and community members) can feel part of a shared identity, objective, sense of belonging.

Maybe that's what is missing in less successful school garden experiences? Maybe we're not reflecting on how culture influences our school garden experiences? Can culture make these experience more authentic, better, easier, more inclusive?

My experience that day with the preps was fulfilling – for me as a teacher, for the children and, given the feedback I received, for parents, too. I'm sure the children all rolled into bed that night after a day of stomping, laughing till their sides hurt, and climbing up and down over the barrels. To be honest, there was just a lot of love. There is even a lot of love in the memory. And maybe that's all it is. Maybe that's all that these school garden or nature experiences within school walls offer – love. Maybe we're all making these experiences too complex, too administrative, too curriculum-driven. Maybe there simply needs to be more love in our school gardens. Just more being. Being still. Being together. Being happy. Isn't that enough?

Maybe not. The idea that school gardens should be spaces of benefit through formal education persists in the dominant discourses. In more recent times, schools are beginning to transform their facilities to include natural environments and thus, more on-site green spaces are created to provide opportunities for children to experience and reap the benefits of gardens (Danks, 2010; Van Dijk-Wesselius et al., 2018). School gardens are part of these green spaces. However, while school gardens are present in schools, there is little evidence to support teacher engagement with school gardens from an informal or interdisciplinary approach in practice (Turner et al., 2014). There are also growing concerns among stakeholders about how to maintain and sustain successful school gardens for students' benefit (Burt et al., 2018; Loftus et al., 2017). We just don't know the who, why or how of teachers' experience of school gardens. What is the meaning of school gardens for teachers? Why would we want to use them? Don't you know teachers are under enough pressure?

Too burnt out to garden

Let's talk about teacher burnout. There are so many reasons why teaching is not the same as it was five, ten or 20 years ago. I know that sounds old-timey but it's true. The teaching profession has become very administrative and this is contributing to teacher burnout. Teachers may experience burnout for a number of reasons: the workload and expectations of teaching has greatly changed over the past few decades. Teachers are often facing heavier workloads that more frequently emphasise paperwork, administrative declarations and meetings. Teaching isn't just about teaching children anymore. The red tape can lead to a lack of teacher autonomy. Teachers simply don't feel that they have the space, time or resources to teach in a way that resonates with them and their teaching philosophy, values and beliefs. And we need these philosophies, values and beliefs to cope with the emotional labour of teaching. Because, let's face it: it is emotionally, intellectually and physically demanding to be a teacher.

I'm sure that some of you have lived this situation: I was at a barbeque one day with many different people I hadn't met before. I was joining into conversations and trying to be social. In one particular sub-circle, there were parents talking about teachers. The parents were saying that 'teachers are lazy', that 'they have too many holidays' and they 'often go on strike for nothing'. It was a difficult conversation to listen to – of course, none of them knew I was a teacher myself. I bided my time and listened as these parents went on to talk about the challenges they were facing with their own children. Later in the conversation, I brought their attention back to what they'd said about teachers being lazy. I said, 'It sounds like you are each facing some challenges as parents. Believe me, I do, too. But can you imagine having 30 children, all with various challenges that you have to deal with for six to seven hours per day, 40 weeks of the year? You mentioned that Jonah has learning difficulties and that homework takes hours. It takes hours for him to do his work at school, too – and we have to manage that against Simon who has finished his work in record time and then spends the rest of the time annoying everyone else. You can imagine that it's challenging, can't you? And that due to the workload, lack of resources, behavioural challenges, pressure from the curriculum and standardised testing, lack of professional autonomy, emotionally demanding nature, sometimes ineffective leadership, inadequate salaries, job insecurity, gaining "points" for tenure, and parental and community pressures, that maybe, just maybe, we might need a couple of weeks' extra holiday a year? And in reality, that holiday is mostly spent lesson planning for the following term – sourcing exciting books, making photocopies, preparing our classrooms. It's exhausting. So, while you are in your own job, where you don't get asked 1000 questions by 30 different children per day, please imagine a world without teachers and you might feel differently about their leave.' Mic drop. Emma out.

I turned heel and retreated. Maybe that was rude. I fell into my partner's arms. 'Let's go,' I whispered. It hadn't been the first time, nor was it the last time, that I'd had that conversation, and I was sick of it. I just couldn't justify it anymore. Teachers need appreciation. And, to be honest, we probably need more help, too. Not because we're helpless, but because we're vocational – we want to serve and support young ones to thrive. That's why it is important that this book asks questions about your own experiences. The teacher's voice is so important – it's time to ask what's actually happening in school gardens through your own perspectives and experiences. Will the real teachers please stand up?

Moving back to 'simple'

It's true: the curriculum and the ever-changing teaching environment may make school gardens more challenging for us to prioritise and implement. However, we teachers may also be making school garden experiences more challenging for ourselves. As I have mentioned, the dominant discourse is around the health and nutritional knowledge outcomes school gardens promote (Ohly et al., 2021). This discourse often acts as a central theme in isolation. Despite the rise of gardening-related themes in the state and national curriculum, our knowledge about the co-construction of school gardens, influenced by social, cultural and contextual factors, remains limited. The research by Taylor et al. (2021) highlights that the discourses of school gardens may be formulated within a hierarchy of power (Wright, 2004). Not all discourses may be considered as equal 'truths' and this has an influence on how school gardens are interpreted and used. Taylor et al. (2021) posit that there may be multiple truths within school gardens. These may be formulated through interactions between social actors but additionally between social actors and the environment (Williams, 2006). Sociocultural and contextual factors play a critical role in understanding school gardens. The discourse around positive health and nutritional outcomes potentially marginalises certain groups of students (Taylor et al., 2021). We don't yet fully understand how meaning is being attributed to school gardens through the interactions of those using it within a particular sociocultural context. By focusing too narrowly on specific outcomes, such as health and nutrition, we may overlook the sociocultural and contextual factors that play a critical role in understanding school gardens. By broadening our perspective and embracing the diverse ways school gardens can be meaningful, we can create more inclusive and enriching experiences for all students.

Journal entry three

How are we using our school garden?

* How is our school garden being used? Is it for curriculum-driven reasons? Or is the interaction more organic, informal and authentic?

* Is the school garden being used to perpetuate a 'power dynamic'? What are the discourses that are present in the garden, and who is benefiting from these discourses? Is the garden being frequently used for marketing, rather than by the children and teachers?

* How can I suggest we use the school garden moving forward?

* What are the cultural influences in our sociocultural context that we could incorporate into our school garden experiences? How might we make our garden a cultural space?

ACTION PLAN

Evaluate the power dynamics and discourses in the garden

Assess whether the school garden is being used to perpetuate a power dynamic. Reflect on the discourses present in the garden and who benefits from these discourses. For instance, consider if the garden is primarily used for showcasing the school to parents and visitors rather than for the educational and social benefit of the students and teachers. Analyse whether the current use of the garden aligns with the values and needs of the entire school community.

Engage with the community

Involve the broader school community, including students, teachers, parents and local residents, in discussions about the garden. Hold meetings or workshops to gather input and suggestions on how the garden can be used more effectively and inclusively. Ensure that all voices are heard and that the garden reflects the diverse cultural and social backgrounds of the community.

Identify cultural influences

Identify the cultural influences present in your sociocultural context that could be incorporated into your school garden experiences. Consider how the garden can become a cultural space that reflects the heritage and traditions of the community. For example, you might plant culturally significant plants or use the garden for cultural celebrations and educational activities related to the community's history.

Promote informal and organic interactions

Encourage more informal and organic interactions in the garden. Allow students to explore and engage with the garden outside of structured class times. Promote the garden as a space for relaxation, play and spontaneous learning. Provide opportunities for students to take ownership of garden projects, fostering a sense of responsibility and connection to the space.

Develop intergenerational programs

Create programs that involve different generations, similar to the grape picking and crushing activity mentioned earlier. Invite older members of the community to share their knowledge and experiences with students in the garden. These interactions can provide valuable learning opportunities and help build a sense of community and continuity.

FOUR

NURTURING RESILIENCE

STRESSORS AND THE SCHOOL GARDEN

In the previous chapter we discussed why teachers may not be engaging with school gardens. However, this discourse that targets teachers as 'responsible' does not consider that we all have a responsibility to our children and communities. Teacher workload is an area for serious concern, and is also recognised as an issue by members of the public. However, there is a gap between the public perception – that teachers are respected and trusted – and teachers, who do not always feel appreciated for their work (Heffernan et al., 2019). These feelings of unappreciation can influence teacher concerns over health, safety and wellbeing, impacting their ability to remain in the profession. Teacher stress is real, and as a society we must move away from the 'teachers need to do more' approach to a 'how can we be part of the solution' approach.

Stressors can be experienced on an individual, collective or societal level. The concept of salutogenesis focuses on understanding, managing and developing meaning from a situation to affront the stressors, using your general resistance resources and moving towards a positive outcome (Antonovsky, 1987). In life, people will all experience stressors – it is one of the guarantees of being human. The stressors that teachers may experience could be psychological, physical or biochemical (Mittelmark et al., 2016; Mittelmark et al., 2022). These stressors cannot always be avoided as they form part of life experiences, but it's important to note that they may cause an internal stress response for the individual that negatively impacts their ability to engage with school gardens (Stoltz & Schaffer, 2018). Individuals who are able to cope with these stressors will be more capable of engagement with the school garden, and more open to feeling fulfilled by the experience (Buch, 2006). Those individuals who are less able to cope with life stressors will be consumed by the stress and potentially disengage with school gardens as a result.

Responses to stressors vary between individuals, and contribute to how they react to the constraints of school gardens (Wethington, 2005). This explains how teachers with similar school garden contexts may have varied perspectives and experiences, based on how they understand, manage and make meaning of their school garden (Vinje et al., 2017). By applying the salutogenesis approach to school gardens, we can explore the contributing factors that support teachers to navigate the stressors associated with school gardens (Mittelmark et al., 2022). We can explore how, despite experiencing similar stressors, some teachers make school gardens 'work' as well as can reasonably be expected. After all, some engagement may be better than no engagement, and shifting the focus from the 'right' type of engagement to the engagement that fits you and your sociocultural context might be a better and more productive way to approach school garden engagement.

The stressors of a school garden

School gardens present many promising benefits for students, while simultaneously presenting stressors for teachers (Burt et al.,

2018). It makes sense that these stressors are many and varied given that pedagogical factors for engaging with school gardens are influenced by multiple factors – from cognitive systems (Falk et al., 2001) to social context (Devine, 2005) to the physical environment (Popkin et al., 2005). Teachers experience increasing pressure in their profession (Kim et al., 2022). Curriculum pressure, time, teacher confidence and skill, training, costs and resources are all barriers to the success of school garden education in schools (Marchant et al., 2019). School garden education focuses on the curriculum-integrated use of school gardens for teaching and learning purposes (Marchant et al., 2019). Even within the current understanding of what a school garden is or should be, there are already several stressors that relate to school gardens as an educational tool (Marchant et al., 2019). Therefore, simply telling teachers to engage with school gardens will not work, nor should it, as this again places the responsibility of school gardens squarely on the shoulders of teachers alone. Rather, we need to first understand the stressors that relate to school gardens within a particular sociocultural context, and then imagine solutions of how each key stakeholder of the school garden can contribute their skills, time and knowledge to support positive school garden initiatives.

In Australia, the national curriculum outlines that students have 'positive relationships with others, and the environment through interaction with the natural world' as 'these relationships are essential for the wellbeing and sustainability of individuals, society and our environment' (Australian Curriculum Assessment and Reporting Authority, 2023). While there is no strict requirement for schools to have a school garden to meet the minimum curriculum requirements, there is a kitchen garden design project in the Year 6 curriculum that potentially implies a formalised, curriculum-driven approach to school gardens. While not specifically mandating school gardens, the Australian Curriculum does provide the directive that students should have contact with the natural world, and school gardens are often one of the few green spaces within school boundaries. While the Australian Curriculum highlights the importance of school gardens, there is a focus on positive relationships and environmental sustainability. The emphasis on formal, structured and curriculum-driven uses of school gardens, notably the Year 6 kitchen garden design project, potentially overshadows the use and benefits of school gardens for alternative reasons or the ways in which teachers attribute meaning to school gardens in practice. Perhaps school gardens are being used informally for reasons that are not currently understood but that are equally beneficial? Furthermore, the curriculum explicitly highlights school gardens as a directive for students to have contact with the natural world (Australian Curriculum Assessment and Reporting Authority, 2023). While this is commendable, it raises questions about whether the broader spectrum of reasons supporting and justifying the importance of school gardens is adequately acknowledged within the curriculum. Research has demonstrated that school gardens are effective in increasing fruit and vegetable intake (Somerset et al., 2005). While the focus on fruit and vegetable intake is positive, maybe school gardens can be used for other reasons that are also (equally, or more) beneficial for a broader range of key stakeholders.

Curriculum and time pressure

Curriculum pressure has been noted as a stressor for teachers in relation to school gardens. In a study conducted in Queensland, Somerset et al. (2005) surveyed teachers in 13 school garden programs. The study demonstrated that even the most enthusiastic teachers have concerns about curriculum stressors:

> *Pressure from the Department of Education to improve academic outcomes is a concern. If resources were spent on a literacy teacher this may happen, but this may take resources away from the kitchen-garden program... Teachers know that the program is making a difference but this is difficult to demonstrate in terms of hard data. (Block et al., 2012)*

A lack of planning and time is a curriculum pressure that creates the perception that school garden use would take away from instructional time (Taylor, 2021). Curriculum and time stressors can contribute to teacher burnout and a lack of desire to engage with the school garden (Yu, 2012). But what if we just needed to rethink the way in which we use school gardens? Maybe the use of the garden isn't necessarily curriculum-driven, but rather, informal and spontaneous – leading to refined focus on self-determination, mindfulness, connection and enjoyment.

Lack of confidence in gardening skills and knowledge

A lack of teacher confidence in their gardening skills and knowledge is a stressor (Greer et al., 2019). When I have spoken to teachers about school gardens, I've noticed an apparent 'imposter syndrome'. Some teachers don't see themselves as knowledgeable or skilled enough to be able to engage with the school garden. I remember speaking to a young teacher who was relatively new to the teaching profession and she said that, while she would love to engage with the garden, as a young teacher and quite new to the school she didn't feel that she had a 'right' to use the school garden. She went on to say that the garden was close to the Year 1 classrooms and that she thought it was 'their thing', and she didn't want to be stepping on anyone's toes. She, therefore, didn't engage with the garden at all – even though she had some excellent ideas of how maths could be taught in the garden by observing spider's webs (of which there were a lot in this particular garden). Totally unprompted, she spoke to me with enthusiasm about the geometric shapes that were visible in spider's webs. She loved the idea of the imperfection and surprise of the shapes that could be found in these intricate patterns, and the potential of sharing that with her students. We spoke about how her students could observe the webs within the garden but also photograph them to take back to the classroom, and use the interactive whiteboard to trace the geometric forms and see the various shapes, angles and mathematics that existed in nature. I shared that there were some great resources from the Aboriginal and Torres Strait Islander Mathematics Alliance, and that it was important to have representation for all children in her classroom – bringing cultural capital into the classroom can enrich everyone's learning.

It struck me that this enthusiastic teacher had a lot of ideas about how to integrate her love of maths teaching and the garden, but remained very reserved, stating that she also didn't want to do anything that could be frowned upon by others. She thought that if other teachers, students and parents saw her out in the garden 'having fun', they might think that she wasn't really working. Despite the strength of her ideas of what she could do in the garden, ironically (or not), she still felt that she didn't have enough skills to be able to take her students into the garden. I've observed these feelings of unease quite a lot in my informal discussions with teachers. Teachers stress that they are uncertain how to integrate the school garden into their teaching (Eames-Sheavly, 1994; Skelly and Zajicek, 1998). However, rather than this being a stress, this may be an opportunity for teachers to use school gardens in other, potentially more flexible, ways that more appropriately fit their sociocultural context.

Insufficient funding and people power

The underutilisation of school gardens is justified by both real and perceived factors (Burt et al., 2018). The perceived stress in relation to school gardens may explain why not all schools have school gardens, or why school gardens that are present may be considered inoperative (Miller, 2007). Funding for the school garden is a stressor, as schools don't usually have the budget to prioritise school garden establishment and maintenance (Yu, 2012). Even after the initial set-up phase, school gardens require additional resources for their continued operation (Somerset et al., 2005).

When I discussed this with a deputy principal, she shared that she felt stressed by all the other competing priorities within the school that also desperately needed funds. She mentioned the rebuilding of an old hall that needed attention (and, therefore, funding to repair it) just to fulfil the school's health and safety requirements. She said that the idea of a school garden, and admittedly the one that they currently had, were great in theory – but that in practice, maintaining the garden in terms of funding and people power was extremely challenging. She shared there had recently been a staff meeting to decide the fate of the school garden. She presented the issue of the garden to the teachers as, ultimately, she didn't want leadership to be responsible for the closure of the school garden. However, she also said that leadership could not continue to bear the burden of the garden on their own. She put it to the teaching team that if they wanted to keep the school garden, they had to find a way of using it. The teachers decided that opening the garden at one of the recreational breaks was the best way to use the garden. They set up a rotating roster where teachers would spend some of the recreational break time in the school garden – but again, this places more pressure squarely on teachers' shoulders. Maybe there are other ways that we can support school gardens?

It's important to note that teachers can't face all the stressors of school on their own. There needs to be a concerted effort by multiple stakeholders within the community to share the load. This will ensure that the school garden is built and managed with and by the people that it serves, and meets the needs of that particular sociocultural context and is emblematic of the school community identity.

Nurturing resilience and wellbeing in children

As discussed earlier in this book, with the rise of household technology, children experience more indoor-based play than any previous generation (James 2007; Larson et al. 2011). And, in our busy lives, time for outdoor engagement is also limited. Eighty per cent of preschool-aged children with employed parents are in a formal early childhood setting for an average of 40 hours a week (Herbst, 2022). Children experience more time in formalised educational settings than ever before, and yet, the use (not the presence) of the outdoors as a 'natural classroom' has decreased due to inflexible frameworks, rigid curriculum and the fear of negative experiences – whether that be the pressure of demanding parents or the risk of accident (James, 2007). Children are, therefore, experiencing a 'nature deficit' (Louv, 2009).

Interactions with nature spaces are important to supporting child development and wellbeing (Elliott, 2010; Wilson, 2012). Educational spaces contribute to child nature connectedness opportunities (Gandini, 1998). However, while there has been increasing efforts to incorporate nature into early childhood settings (Keeler, 2008; Moore & Cooper-Marcus, 2008; Sobel, 2008), these nature spaces are somewhat underutilised in some circumstances (Miller et al., 2009). The types of nature and interaction available to children in school settings will have an impact on the depth of their nature connectedness. Strong nature connectedness in childhood has been demonstrated to improve connection to the natural world as adults (Chawla, 2009; Lozzi, 1989).

While natural outdoor spaces present opportunities for improved child wellbeing and learning outcomes, some educators are more successful than others in providing deep nature connectedness opportunities for children. Educators' explicit and implicit beliefs guide their actions and practices in the educational setting (Richardson, 1994). Opportunities and limitations of the educational setting also influence practice (Herzog, 2002). Importantly, other stakeholders, such as parents and community members, could also play an integral role in ensuring everyone gets the most out of school garden experiences.

How do we strengthen our communities to better support school gardens? How do we ensure school gardens don't become too challenging, too time-consuming, too much?

Journal entry four

How do stressors impact our school garden experience?

- What stressors do I experience as a teacher in relation to our school garden?
- What stressors do I see other stakeholders (leadership, parents, students, community members) experiencing?
- What resources might we need to overcome these stressors?

ACTION PLAN

Identify stressors

Begin by reflecting on the stressors you experience in relation to the school garden. Document your personal stressors, whether they are psychological, physical or biochemical. Consider the stressors you observe in other stakeholders, such as school leadership, parents, students and community members. Recognise that these stressors might vary widely between individuals and groups.

Conduct a stakeholder survey

Create and distribute a survey to gather input from all stakeholders involved with the school garden. Ask questions that help identify their stressors, perceptions and ideas for improvement. This will provide a comprehensive understanding of the challenges faced by different members of the school community in relation to the garden.

Host a stakeholder meeting

Organise a meeting with representatives from all stakeholder groups. Share the results of the survey and facilitate a discussion on the identified stressors. Encourage open communication and brainstorming to develop collaborative solutions. Focus on building a supportive community around the school garden.

Develop a collaborative plan

Based on the survey and meeting insights, develop a collaborative action plan to address the identified stressors. Ensure that the plan includes contributions from all stakeholders, leveraging their unique skills, time and knowledge. This shared responsibility approach can help alleviate the burden on teachers and promote a sense of community ownership.

Provide professional development

Arrange professional development opportunities for teachers to build their confidence and skills in using the school garden. Workshops or training sessions can cover topics such as gardening basics, integrating garden activities into the curriculum, and managing outdoor classrooms. Empower teachers with the knowledge and tools they need to feel capable and enthusiastic about using the garden. Where possible, engage experienced members of the community to run these sessions.

Create informal garden opportunities

Encourage informal and spontaneous use of the school garden. Allow students and teachers to explore and engage with the garden outside of structured class times. Promote the garden as a space for relaxation, play and unplanned learning. This can reduce the pressure on teachers to always have a structured plan and allow for more organic interactions.

Seek funding and resources

Identify potential funding sources to support the establishment and maintenance of the school garden. This could include grants, community fundraisers or partnerships with local businesses and organisations. Allocate resources efficiently to ensure the garden remains sustainable without placing undue stress on any one group.

Integrate cultural elements

Incorporate cultural elements into the garden to reflect the sociocultural context of your school community. Plant culturally significant species, celebrate cultural events in the garden, and invite community members to share their cultural practices and knowledge. This can enhance the garden's relevance and inclusivity.

Implement a rotating garden duty schedule

Develop a rotating schedule for garden maintenance and supervision that includes teachers, parents and community volunteers. This shared responsibility approach ensures that no single group is overwhelmed and promotes broader community involvement.

FIVE

GUARDIANS OF GROWTH

THE ROLE OF PASSIONATE TEACHERS AND ENTHUSIASTIC SUPPORTERS

'The scarecrow's clothes change regularly. This week it's Book Week, so they have a superhero costume on; last week they had a ski jacket for our Winter Wonderland day; next week, who knows?'

I was at an on-site visit as part of my research into school gardens, and the teacher I was walking with was discussing the scarecrow that reigns over the school garden from the far corner. I shared a smile with her. As I took in the superhero scarecrow I wondered, *who are the true superheros here?* As I furthered my research it was becoming clear to me that the responsibility for school gardens often falls, fairly or unfairly, upon the shoulders of a self-elected hero: the Passionate Teacher.

The passion that drives the key teacher role may be established by a sense of opportunity, rather than any source currently present in the garden. The key teacher is exhibiting situated agency. Situated agency is the capacity of an individual to act and make decisions within a specific context. Situated agency recognises that humans are active in engaging with their environment: shaping it and being shaped by it.

I broke my smile and looked up at the scarecrow again. At first, it seemed they were standing alone. It made me think that the Passionate Teacher, much like the scarecrow, can surely not succeed in the school garden as efficiently on its own. It must have help. As I looked around I saw CDs from the 90s hanging from the nearby trees – an eclectic disco ball of No Doubt, Alanis Morrisette and Madonna's *Greatest Hits*. To me they looked like the scarecrow's back-up dancers, glistening in the sunlight. Indeed, the scarecrow was obviously not a lone operator; they needed the support of these CDs to ward off the birds with their prying eyes. My attention turned back to the teacher who was giving me the tour, as she interjected: 'The teacher who changes the scarecrow's clothes is the main driver of this school garden. She just enjoys the garden and chatting to the children of all different grades on her lunchbreak.' It was then I realised: this teacher is the Passionate Teacher.

The Passionate Teacher understands that their teaching stretches beyond a one-size-fits-all approach. They have a strong sense of situated agency, and have been instrumental and proactive in engaging with the diverse needs of their students. I could tell through the storytelling of the teacher I was with that the Passionate Teacher appears to feel empowered by the meaning that is co-constructed within the sociocultural context of their school garden.

I glanced back at the CDs and the scarecrow as we finished our tour. Indeed, the Passionate Teacher is not alone. The circular shapes of the CDs reminded me of the interpretivist loop within which individuals operate in a school, shaping the learning environment while simultaneously being shaped by it. The stakeholders who interact with and within the garden influence the garden's meaning, and the meaning of the garden, in turn, influences the stakeholders.

It is a cycle of generation and regeneration of meaning within the school garden.

The teacher who was guiding me that day had a role to play, too. The task of teacher-colleagues is to advocate for and support the school garden. The combination of the key teacher role and the supportive teacher-colleague role is a determinant of success. Supporting teacher-colleagues may want the school garden to work, but don't necessarily like gardening or want to participate in the garden themselves.

This demonstrates that there is a division of tasks that occurs in schools that manage successful school garden projects. Everyone has their own task, and that's what contributes to making the school garden work. However, this division of roles seems to happen organically – no one is told what their role is. Teachers usually self-elect into one of three roles:

1. The Passionate Teacher
2. Active supporters: a small group of teachers who are active in the garden
3. Non-active supporters: teacher-colleagues who support the garden, but are not actively involved.

Of course, you would also have teachers who are not supportive of the garden and are therefore not involved.

The other teachers are able to leverage the Passionate Teacher's enthusiasm without everyone having to take on the key responsibility of school garden management and maintenance themselves. This means that there is both a distributed action, as one, or a few, key teachers drive the school garden project, and also a concerted action on the level of the teacher-colleagues to support the main teacher(s). Concerted action is an important element of school garden success. Regardless of the configuration of the driving group, whether it's one individual teacher or a small group of teachers, the commonality is that the key teachers all have a personal passion for the garden.

The Passionate Teacher

So, where does passion for school gardens come from? In my discussions with teachers, it appears that our drive to be actively involved in the school garden stems from our own passions that are peripheral to gardening or nature in some way – but these personal interests are not universal. Some key teachers are driven by their love for gardening; some love the serenity of the garden; some love the space as a 'meeting place'; others love sciences such as biology or biodiversity; and some are driven by the biophilia (connection with nature) they feel in the garden.

I have been the Passionate Teacher of many school gardens. My involvement was driven by my natural curiosity: I want to see, do, touch, taste, feel, hear, be and experience all that there is in this world. And this curiosity extends to plants.

After my husband and I married we went exploring on a family trip with my parents, my two siblings and their partners. We hired a minibus and we drove through countryside France. On the one hand it sounds idyllic: visiting lavender fields and eating goat cheese straight from the farm. On the other, we were trapped as an adult family of eight on a bus for hours at a time. We drove through gorges while my father grasped the overhanging handle, telling us we were driving too fast, too close to the middle, too close to the edge. It did get a little tedious at times. Thankfully, our wonderful children were not born yet – can you imagine eight adults plus six boys aged ten and under? It would have been hectic.

Anyway, on this trip, I noticed a long vegetable garden hugging the roadside at the entrance of a quaint stone-walled French village. A little further along the road there was a small A-frame chalkboard marked simply with the word *déjeuner* – lunch. I was driving at the time, so had the power to stop, which I did. I pulled us over just in front of the chalkboard sign and we walked back along the narrow road to the vegetable garden. It grew wildly, but it was the best organised chaos I'd ever seen. Pumpkins provided flashes of colour in among a thick, dense blanket of a green weed-like plant – I had no idea what it was as I had never seen it before. The tops of leeks stood like an army of white and green soldiers, with apple trees stretching high above them like generals. The garden was wild and crazy and delightful.

We wandered back to the chalkboard, which had a single, solid, heavy red door adjacent. There was a bell above it, which chimed as I pushed the door open. I was not quite sure what I would see behind it. From the exterior the building looked like a farmhouse, someone's home, and certainly not somewhere that was open to the public. But beyond that door, much like the garden outside, was another world. It was dark inside, but animated. It seemed like all of the village came together to eat here every day. And, while they could have had an eye on us as eight foreigners, six of us of non-French-speaking, invading their space for lunch, they didn't. The raucous laughing, slamming of weathered hands on tables and back-slapping continued.

An older woman with long grey hair half-fastened with a flat clip came up to us with a palm-sized notebook to take our order. There weren't any menus. She spoke to us in French and we could ascertain that there was a soup and that it was green – *très bien*! Eight bowls of dark green soup quickly appeared in eight different-sized, coloured and shaped bowls. It appeared that I, with my long golden hair still plaited from our wedding, was now Goldilocks and we had arrived at the home of the three bears – the long-haired woman and two jovial farmers who obviously believed the rule that it was midday somewhere, even though it was really only about 11am. The woman said *devinez*, which means 'guess', so we proceeded to guess the vegetables in the soup. Zucchini? No. Broccoli? No. Beans? No. Capsicum? No. Peas? No. Cucumber, brussels sprouts, spinach, asparagus, cabbage, leek, fennel, celery, green tomatoes, artichoke, green onions? No. Kale? No, but closer.

It was a leaf, she told us, and said that we would have seen it in her garden. She was making hand actions that seemed to say that it covered the ground. She kept saying *partout* which means 'everywhere'. Ah – the knee-high leafed plants that we'd seen blanketing the garden! She instructed me to go and see it again and come back and report on what it looked like to my family. I did. What I noticed was that part of the leaf seemed to have small hairs. She made a motion to communicate that they *pique* – sting. Aha! Stinging nettle. We were eating stinging nettle soup. I swear my family members' faces dropped just a little bit, and 'oohs and aahs' that were just a bit too enthusiastic to be genuine ensued. It's funny how your mind plays up when you know what something is made of – it seemed to change the taste (at least in our heads). But objectively, despite the very dark green colour, it was actually delicious.

This event was one of the most memorable experiences I have had with gardens. Gardens don't have to be manicured, straight-edged and 'proper' – they can be authentic, inspiring and have a personality of their own. I think once we take some of that perfectionism out of gardens, their use and the whole experience becomes much more pleasant for everyone.

You don't have to be the Passionate Teacher to make a difference. The supporting teachers who speak positively about the garden, and about the Passionate Teacher leading it, is also important. These roles may also evolve over time. A Passionate Teacher may become a supporting teacher and vice versa. If you are the Passionate Teacher now, that doesn't mean you always have to be – these roles are not rooted in the soil.

The Passionate Teacher may also derive their passion from a number of different places, and may also be from any discipline – music, art, sport, maths, languages. The Passionate Teacher does not have to be a science teacher, because what teachers are actually doing in school gardens is not always science-related. The Passionate 'Teacher' may not even be a teacher but a trusted member of the community who has been invited into the school to drive the school garden project – an enthusiastic parent, caregiver, grandparent or local resident may be a positive 'key' person for your school garden.

Active supporters

It is important that the 'key' person driving the garden has support from a small group of active participants, and that a larger group of non-active, but supportive people speak positively about that garden. We have to make sure the discourse isn't lip service – of course, it is positive that the school garden is used as a marketing tool to boost their enrolments, but there has to be an authentic and genuine care for the garden and the benefits it provides, too.

Our gardens may have turned into disarray through school closures during the pandemic, or for other reasons. However, today is a new day, and it's time to turn over a new leaf (pun intended – I honestly can't help myself). As evidenced by my stinging nettle soup story, sometimes organised chaos produces great results. Things don't always have to be perfect to be great, rewarding, inspirational, fun and heartfelt. The garden should simply reflect the sociocultural community that it serves. That is where the active supporters come into play.

Active supporters can manifest in a range of different ways. One of the best ways to gather them is through a working bee. In some cases there may not be strong ties between the school and its community for all the reasons mentioned earlier in this book (busy work schedules, children's extracurricular activities, living in urban environments and so on). So it may be challenging for the school body to identify interested supporters on its own, and this is where a coming-together may be useful.

Of course, a coming-together could be organised in a very structured manner, via parents and carer's meetings, focus groups, officially interviewing or surveying the local community about the school garden, or gathering quantitative data about the demographics of the school community – ethnicity, housing, family composition, income and so on. Or we could just extend an invitation to the school community to come in and help out in the garden.

Observing the interactions, conversations, roles and sociocultural complexities presenting at a coming-together may also help us to understand our school garden. The garden itself might also show you its personality. One garden that I visited had capucine (nasturtium) flowers running wild – a vibrant yellow and orange! The garden felt like an active space, where laughing, talking, excitement and wonder were highly encouraged. Simply creating that link, inviting people in, talking, working side-by-side and being together creates a living garden space. And we all know that, post-pandemic, being together is pretty all right.

The only issue that I have noticed with working bees is that it is often the same people, often parents, who put up their hand to volunteer every time. These parents must be celebrated for going above and beyond their regular parenting duties to give their time and effort to support their community. Interestingly, when I have spoken to other parents who did not volunteer in the garden, I realised that their lack of volunteering was not due to unavailability or unwillingness, but often due to their own perceptions of self. They didn't think they had the skills necessary to contribute to a school garden working bee, or believed that others had more of these skills and that, therefore, their help was not needed or as valuable as what others could offer.

So, when you extend an invitation to potential active supporters, make it clear that they don't need to be a gardener to make a valuable contribution. Schools actually need the help of all different types of people; and, as we have already explored, school gardens are not only places for gardening and the sciences. They are places for story time (both listening and writing), conversations, just 'being' – potentially in the form of yoga, meditation or a routine 'sit spot'. You can make music or art or play sport in the school garden. All of this requires the support of many different parents, with varying skills, at varying levels.

Even if you are not a gardener, gardens are for you, too.

When I mentioned working bees to one of my colleagues at university, she said that she was one of the parents who couldn't volunteer, and didn't want to be villainised for that. She worked full-time and was a single mother, and it was challenging to juggle this. She said she often wasn't available at the times that the school needed volunteers and that, if an opportunity did fall on a weekend when she was available, she wasn't inclined to show up because she also needed time to rest and recuperate from a hectic week. All of this is understandable. People shouldn't feel that they *have to* contribute or risk being criticised. However, they should always feel welcome. Just as school gardens should be welcoming and accessible spaces for all children, parents should equally feel as though these spaces are welcoming and accessible. Consequently, it is important to host working bees with a choice of day – maybe having a working bee on a Friday afternoon after school, followed by another one the next morning, would suit a greater range of parents and families.

Encouraging parents to bring their children to help can also create an atmosphere of unity and joint parent-children experiences as memories. One school that I visited encouraged parents to bring all their children, even younger ones, and had a teacher present to watch younger children while the parents and primary-school-aged children helped out in the garden. Again, whatever the configuration of your working bee, it has to suit the sociocultural complexities of your school and school community.

Non-active supporters

In addition to active supporters, it appears that school gardens also need non-active, but still positive, supporters. These are people who champion the garden, sing its praises and appreciate its presence, without actively contributing themselves.

This concept may appear confusing. Why would you want to encourage someone simply to be happy that the garden is there without them ever lifting a finger themselves to contribute to the space? Well, because what you *don't* want are negative contributors – people who complain about the garden, don't see its benefits and would prefer it to be filled in and grassed over. Mowing an expansive lawn is so much easier, after all – and it's much more cost-effective. And believe me, I have seen this happen. I had some involvement with a school that had a small school garden. The garden had probably been quite beautiful at one point, quite some time ago. I could feel some bricked edging underneath the overgrown weeds. Once a year, tulips would pop up sporadically, creating a living dot-to-dot of colour. The tulips were vulnerable as their fragile stems poked out of the ground with enough time to be prodded, broken and picked. It was, after all, a garden for three- to six-year-old children – baby Godzillas. The tulips never really stood a chance. This particular garden ended up being paved over. 'More room for the tricycles,' they said. 'More entertainment for the children.' I'm sure the bees were left thinking, 'Am I not pretty enough?'

Gardens can be wild and unkept, but there seems to be more appreciation for the garden when it reflects the community in which it is situated. In the case of the garden that was paved over, members of the community were not consulted. This brings us back to the point that the school garden must have advocators – people who speak positively about and appreciate its use. The best-case scenario is that most of the school community would speak positively about the school garden – however, this cannot occur unless they have some knowledge of or access to the garden. As such, it might be an idea to keep the garden open during parent-teacher interviews or open days, with someone present to discuss what's happening in the garden and how that reflects your school community. Communicating what's happening in the garden via the parent newsletter might also be a viable option to increase buy-in and positive perception.

Ultimately, the school garden should be for everyone.

Journal entry five

Who supports our garden?

- Who do I think is the key driver of our school garden – the Passionate Teacher?
- Where do I think their passion for the school garden comes from?
- What are my passions? How might that shape my interaction with the school garden?
- Who are the garden's active supporters? Why those people? What do they contribute?
- Are there parents or other community members who might want to contribute to the school garden but don't know how? Who are they? What might be restricting their involvement?
- What do families and local community members say about our school garden? Do we have positive supporters?

ACTION PLAN

Understand your Passionate Teacher

Start by identifying the key driver(s) of your school garden. Reflect on who these individuals are and where their passion for the school garden stems from. Engage in a conversation with them to understand their motivations, challenges and aspirations for the garden.

Leverage your own passions

Reflect on your own passions and consider how they might shape your interaction with the school garden. Determine whether you can align your personal interests with garden activities, whether it's through gardening, organising events, teaching subjects related to the garden, or simply spending time in the garden with students.

Engage active supporters

Identify and engage the garden's active supporters. Understand what these individuals contribute and why they are involved. Facilitate regular meetings or informal gatherings to maintain enthusiasm and share responsibilities. Encourage them to take on specific roles that match their strengths and interests.

Address barriers for potential volunteers

Identify parents or community members who might want to contribute to the school garden but are currently not involved. Reach out to these individuals to understand what is restricting their involvement. This could be due to time constraints, lack of gardening knowledge or perceived inadequacy. Provide flexible opportunities for participation, such as weekend working bees, and offer training or mentorship to build confidence.

Host inclusive working bees

Organise regular working bees to encourage community involvement. Offer flexible timings to accommodate different schedules, such as a Friday evening followed by a Saturday morning. Encourage families to bring their children, creating an atmosphere of unity and shared experiences. Ensure that these events are welcoming to all, regardless of gardening expertise. (I'll talk more about the specifics of working bees in chapter 6.)

Create informal engagement opportunities

Encourage informal and spontaneous use of the school garden. Allow students and teachers to explore and engage with the garden outside of structured class times. Promote the garden as a space for relaxation, play and unplanned learning.

Foster non-active positive supporters

Identify and cultivate non-active but positive supporters. These individuals might not actively participate in gardening activities, but can advocate for the garden, speak positively about it and appreciate its presence. Engage these supporters through regular updates and invite them to garden-related events.

Utilise open days and parent-teacher events

Keep the garden open during parent-teacher events or open days with a knowledgeable person present to discuss the garden's activities and its importance. This can help increase awareness and appreciation among parents and the local community. Use these opportunities to gather feedback and ideas from parents and community members.

*

SIX

GROWING TOGETHER

PEER-TO-PEER CONNECTION

'My name is Arthur. Can I be/play/sit with you, please?'

We've moved countries a few times with our children. Each time our children integrate into a new school environment, I encourage them to focus on connection with other students in their first week. We've often discussed the line, 'My name is Arthur. Can I be/play/sit with you, please?' It's an ice-breaker, a way in to give them at least one connection in their day that helps them to feel less alone as they transition to a new school.

School gardens are excellent places for children to make these connections, because the spaces are diverse, evolutionary and dynamic. As teachers, we must recognise that school gardens may be lifelines for some students – and without them, they simply can't bridge that gap into friendships.

Children's experiences of school gardens

My own research has demonstrated that school gardens are indeed diverse spaces. Teachers have told me the range of students that were self-electing to use school garden spaces was varied. Some students lived in public housing, some in standalone houses with big backyards. Children in urban, coastal and rural areas all spend time in school gardens.

As I mentioned in chapter 2, some scholars have argued that children from different socioeconomic backgrounds may not feel welcome in the school garden. However, in the research that I conducted across three case study schools, this was not shown to be the case. Children from all socioeconomic backgrounds in a range of residential areas and housing situations were all engaging voluntarily with the school garden on their lunchbreaks in the schools I studied. Of course, this does not mean that this will be true in all cases – there may be some sociocultural context in which particular groups of students may feel isolated or segregated from the school garden. This reiterates how important it is to collaborate with your key stakeholders to have a school garden that is representative of your sociocultural context so that everyone can feel that this space is welcoming and accessible for the enjoyment of all.

One of the school gardens I visited had a 'buddy bench', where children could sit when they were actively or unconsciously looking for a friend – or, at the very least, someone to spend that lunchtime with. Children were told that they could go and sit on the bench if they were alone, and that they were never really alone in the garden as there were always one or two other students in the vicinity, interacting with the garden or each other in the way that they deemed appropriate or that gave them meaning. Having the buddy bench in the school garden also protected children from view somewhat, meaning they could sit on the bench without fear of ridicule from their peers for 'having no friends'. The rhetoric and teacher discourse about the bench also made it a widely accepted phenomenon within the school. Even children who did have friends sat there at times to 'take a break' from the big expansive spaces of the ovals or the loud noises of the undercover areas or handball courts. School gardens are great places for children to seek solace on their own or connection with others.

The multi-age 'in between' space

The school gardens I visited for my research were all open at lunchtime and were multi-age, meaning that children from any year level could come and enjoy them. The teachers I spoke with shared how they often witnessed siblings in the garden together (sometimes playing together, sometimes not) and that they felt that siblings were comforted by each other's presence within a small radius in among the expansive spaces of the school. This was particularly true in the initial stages of the year where younger siblings had joined the school or where families were new to the school community. The school garden in this sense provided a 'gateway' space: an area to enjoy lunchtime and meet other students, but without being flung into the chaos and expanse of an oval or basketball court (but equally, not an inside space such as a library or computer lab). The school garden is where it is at, the ultimate 'in between' space. It is where lunchtime dreams are planted and where friendships and kinships blossom – all while avoiding the whizzing of stray frisbees!

In addition to kin relationships, teachers also commented that they saw inter-age friendships bloom in the school garden. One of the deputy principals I spoke with shared that she often saw older students taking responsibility and developing their leadership skills in the garden by assisting younger students. She was quick to add that this didn't mean that the older students told the younger students what to do or guided them towards particular activities; rather, the younger students were self-guided and chose how they interacted with the garden with the older students as incidental support. Often, older and younger students would just chat while they were in the garden. Sometimes the students were just 'being', and sometimes they were participating in an activity. Both were valid ways of engaging with the garden and provided an opportunity to talk. The deputy principal stated that most of the time the conversations started off focused on the activity or the enjoyment of being in the garden itself, but often evolved into chats about other interest areas that had nothing to do with gardens at all. Students started to find commonalities: 'We go on holidays to Bundaberg' would be followed by, 'Oh, I've been there too, to watch the turtles hatching'; or 'I am learning the cello this year but I don't like it' would be followed by, 'Stick with it. I learnt the cello in Year 2 and didn't like it either, but I stuck with it and now I learn the guitar which is much better.' The peer-to-peer connections within the school garden contributed to students feeling that they belonged within the school community. A positive sense of connection and belonging improve our overall wellbeing and encourage us to develop further resources to be able to affront the stressors of life. School gardens are perfect spaces to encourage both connection and belonging in a very informal and familiar environment.

Teacher–student connections: can you hear the people sing?

One of the most interesting themes of meaning that I discovered in my research was that of connection within school gardens. This connection manifested in a variety of ways – sometimes it was peer-to-peer; sometimes student to teacher; sometimes teacher to families; and sometimes school to community. In the variety of ways that it presented, connection was a key theme across the school gardens that I explored in context.

In one of the school gardens that I visited, a teacher would sing with his students in the garden. He would put on music while he was in the garden with the children, and they would sing along. Some would concentrate solely on the singing aspect while others would plant, water or weed while singing on and off. Others would not sing or do any kind of activity but would enjoy the animated environment of the garden. The teacher said he got really good at some of the rap songs with the Year 6 children (which was very much outside of his comfort zone). His face lit up when he was talking about it. He was actually the principal of this school and was in his early 40s. I could see that he also felt liberated by this experience – he said it was his favourite part of the week, and that he cherished these special moments to just 'be'. So, not only were the children enjoying this experience in the school garden and creating a bond with one another, but the teacher was enjoying it, too. He also said that there were some students he had never heard sing who had amazing voices – which he would not have known if they hadn't had the opportunity to sing in the school garden.

Parents as partners

One morning at the beginning of the school year I joined my sister-in-law to drop my five-year-old nephew off to his new school. It was an inner-city primary school in Melbourne's western suburbs. As I walked over astroturf I quite innocently remarked on its presence, potentially laced with some atonement. My sister-in-law picked up on my tone quickly, defending the school: 'They have a grassed field further down the back.' She really never misses a beat.

The astroturf had handball squares and a soccer pitch spray-painted onto it in blue and red. My nephew pointed to a large blue dot and said, 'This is where the soccer ball goes.' I was amused and perplexed. I wondered how he, and all the other kids, would know where to put the ball if it weren't painted on the ground – mandated, required, guided?

We reached a small children's playground. The ground was covered in woodchips, which smelled divine – it was, after all, only the second day of school and still summer. My nephew joined two of his classmates to play. The boys began throwing some of the woodchips onto a low platform. The action stirred up the smell of the natural wood even more and I vocalised my delight in the waves of eucalyptus wafting towards me. I closed my eyes just for a moment to breathe in. This moment of wonderment was interrupted, though, by the mother of one of the other boys. She was helicoptering over her son. 'Don't do that, Marty – the woodchips are for protecting children from falls, not to play with.' *Maybe we should be playing with woodchips?* I pondered. I tried to engage her in conversation about children wearing glasses (as I noticed her son wearing them, and so does my own), but she was distracted – hovering with fervour over Marty's every move, so much so that Marty moved away from the woodchips and the nature play space and towards the plastic fort. The wafts of eucalyptus halted quite suddenly as we snapped back to the plastic and concrete jungle.

Parents are key stakeholders in school garden engagement. Parents understand the benefits of being in nature, but concerns over incidents and strangers, and the helicopter parenting style that is prominent in our society, restricts free, educational experiences in even the smallest nature spaces (Truong et al., 2022). The focus on nature education as 'play' may restrict some key stakeholders from routinely interacting with nature. This is particularly evident as most nature-based experiences have previously been referred to as 'rewilding', which in itself connotes a 'wild' or extreme experience. Focusing on biophilia (connection with nature) as a 'requietening' may provide greater reassurance for parents. The 'requietening' could occur through mindfulness theory (Kabat-Zinn, 2005) and place-based education theory (Anderson, 2017; Nicol, 2020). Maybe children just want to *be* in nature spaces. Maybe parents just want to *be* in nature spaces with their children. Maybe teachers want that, too – just to 'hang out' in the school garden and chat, engaging with students, parents and community members who they might not otherwise have the opportunity to meet.

Supporting the school garden

In the previous chapter we touched on working bees as an excellent way to promote school gardens and extend access to and inclusion within them.

As I was engaging in my research, a single mother said to me that she often felt guilty as she could never attend the working bees that were planned by her daughter's school. She said that they were often held at times when she couldn't attend due to her work in a retail shop. I had heard this from another parent, too: a nurse. He said that shift work made it difficult to commit to a scheduled working bee and that it either had to be planned well in advance (so that he could block the time in his calendar) or would be a last-minute decision (where he could just show up). It highlighted to me that school garden support needed to be flexible to be successful. It also emphasised that the school garden had to consider and cater to the type of community it represented, and that collaboration with the various stakeholders was necessary (which increased investment of time and money to ensure its sustainability over the long-term).

Following are some more of my findings in terms of how support can be sought and given for school gardens through working bees and other means.

Regular intervals and planned schedule

It appeared that one of the solutions to the working bee schedule was to host working bees at regular intervals (rather than only once in a blue moon). This regularity meant that parent volunteers could plan ahead and organise care for their children if needed. As discussed previously, one school that had seemingly successful working bees had one on a Thursday evening after school and another on the following Saturday morning. The benefit of this was that parents who had varied or competing times had the choice to come to either one or the other based on their own schedule and responsibilities.

Task-based working bees

Some schools had task-based working bees where the nature of the task was clearly outlined in the schedule at the beginning of the school year and people could self-elect into the working bee that best suited their skills. The working bee tasks included building garden beds, bird houses and insect hotels, as well as planting, weeding and maintenance.

Desktop and financial support

One school that I visited recognised that not everyone could provide hands-on support. This school wanted to have an inclusive approach to supporting the school garden and therefore shared a list of tasks that could be completed by parent volunteers from their home or workplace. This included writing and applying for grants or preparing letters to local governments or suppliers requesting donations of seeds, tools or signage for the school garden. Some parents were encouraged to form a fundraising group for the garden by seeking sponsorship from local businesses. Another school that I interviewed had set up a partnership with a local disability service that prepared seedlings for planting by the students.

Some parents won't be able to provide time at all, but may be able to make a financial contribution to support the maintenance and supplies needed to keep the school garden viable.

Skills sharing

My son attended a kindergarten program when he was four. At the time, I was a full-time working mum of two boys (our other son was aged two). My partner had taken a ten-month unpaid sabbatical to care for our boys which was very valuable as I was commuting to Brisbane, about 1.5 hours each way, every day. We had swapped our house in France with people around the Sunshine Coast, which meant that we shuffled around about eight times in the ten-month period.

During this time, the kindergarten hosted monthly evening skills sessions on a variety of topics, from parenting skills to guiding behaviour in young children to healthy eating – and there was also one on gardening. The gardening session was hosted by a parent who had recently completed a horticultural certificate and was working with other ex-military personnel who suffered from PTSD.

Gardening was a form of rehabilitation for these ex-soldiers and provided them with a purpose and practical skills to grow their own vegetables. Importantly, the garden also provided them with a place where they could come and connect while at the same time being occupied by an activity. The parent spoke of how being in the garden helped him to voice any mental health challenges he had been facing. He said that he had previously had difficulty speaking about his problems as the context for discussions had been quite static or unfamiliar, and that dissuaded him from opening up to conversations. He said that simply being in the garden helped him feel connected to something bigger than himself. He spoke very vulnerably about the isolation he had experienced since leaving the military and that the connection with both peers and strangers in the garden enabled him to feel that there was a place for him in this life, and that he could learn and share new skills with others. He said that giving this 'talk' was a very new experience for him and that he wasn't sure if he would be able to share in this forum – but he also stated that he wanted others to feel empowered like he did through his experiences in the garden.

This man also shared his experiences of composting, permaculture gardening, and sustainable practices such as building possum and bird houses, insect hotels and water features to divert rainwater into the garden beds. He provided information on gardening skills – but more than that, he highlighted that our shared experiences in a garden, our connections with one another, can strengthen our communities. Connection is an important element of community and school gardens.

Community events

One of the schools that I visited participated in the local agricultural show. They entered their produce in the 'prize vegetables' category of the show, as well as entering the 'create a picture using fresh produce' category, and the arts categories where students would draw, paint or write about their experiences and perspectives of the school garden. This showcased the school garden on a community level, as people could come and observe what the students had been doing in the school garden and how they felt about it through their writing, drawings and paintings. Participating in the show also helped to make the school garden a multidisciplinary space with its use spanning beyond the sciences to the arts, music, literature, languages, history and culture.

This school would also place produce from the school garden at a garden stall for community members and families to take, leaving a small donation in the honesty box as a token of their thanks if they could. As we lived in an area known for its pineapples, the school also held a community harvest festival which was a nod to the history of the school on lands that previously would have been a pineapple plantation farm. Pineapples were hacked into quarters and then slices and passed around like a flotilla of pineapple vessels. It was quick, effortless and quite spontaneous. The school simply communicated to community members to 'come in and have some pineapple' at school pick-up one Thursday afternoon. The festival gave students the opportunity to take their parents into the garden, share some fresh pineapple and chat to other teachers and parents (or their own children) about the garden – but not only the garden! I witnessed teachers engaging with those sometimes reluctant parents to check in and see if everything was okay, in a quest to work collaboratively to support their child. I witnessed parents who had had disagreements come together in the same space and acknowledge each other's presence – potentially a step in the right direction to repairing fractured relationships. I saw all of us using the garden space to understand one another a little better.

Influencers and social media

Another school community I visited had a mum who was a social media 'influencer'. Now, I'll admit that I'm not very well-versed in the world of influencers, but I understood this mum was sharing vlogs about healthy eating, wellbeing, relationships and recipes on social media. She didn't actually do any filming in the garden as that wouldn't have been appropriate, but she often spoke about the school garden in her videos and discussed some of the things the children had been doing and how they related to health and wellness – for example, how to use garden produce in recipes and lunch boxes. While this type of content reflects the more traditional interpretations of school gardens as spaces for growing vegetables and increasing nutritional knowledge, rather than the more nuanced meaning of school gardens that my own research discovered, the mother's influence was valuable and important within the school community.

As I've mentioned before, the school garden has meaning through the interactions and language of the key people who are using the garden. With this in mind, the way in which the garden is celebrated will contribute to its identity and, in turn, the way people use it – it is a cyclical process where the interactions with and within the garden influence each stakeholder which, in turn, influence the interactions with and within the garden.

While we're on the topic of social media, using it to communicate with your school community and the public can help generate interest in your school garden. Let people know what has been going on, how students are using the garden and if there are any important events coming up. Photos and videos let people gain a real feeling of what your garden is about – just be sure not to have any students' faces visible, and only record appropriate content with the consent of parents and teachers. Of course, there are other ways in which you can communicate about your school garden, too – the school newsletter is also a great way to celebrate all the enjoyment that is happening in your school garden.

By actively engaging all key stakeholders – students, teachers, parents, families, caregivers and the broader community – everyone can share in the construction of meaning and identity of the school garden. The school garden can be emblematic of the sociocultural context of the school, co-constructed by and with those who use it regularly.

Journal entry six

What is our garden's identity?

* What is the identity of our school garden – from the sociocultural context and from the garden itself?
* Does our school garden have a personality?
* What would make our school garden more reflective of the community it exists within?

ACTION PLAN

Understand the school garden's identity

Assess the sociocultural context by conducting surveys or holding focus group discussions with students, teachers, parents and community members to understand their perceptions and expectations of the school garden. Analyse the demographic and cultural background of your school community to ensure the garden reflects its diversity. Observe the garden's personality by spending time in the garden, noting different activities, interactions and natural elements that give the garden its unique character. Document these observations through photos, videos or written descriptions.

Foster peer-to-peer connections

Promote inclusivity by implementing strategies such as the 'buddy bench' where students can sit if they are looking for someone to interact with, ensuring that no child feels isolated. Encourage students to use inclusive language and behaviours, such as introducing themselves and inviting others to join them in garden activities. Enable multi-age interactions by allowing students of different grades to interact in the space. Encourage older students to mentor younger ones informally, fostering leadership and social skills. Organise periodic events where siblings and students from different grades can come together to work on garden projects, ensuring a sense of community.

Enhance teacher-student connections

Encourage informal engagement by allocating specific times for teachers to spend in the garden with students, engaging in activities such as storytelling, singing or simply being present. Highlight and share these moments in staff meetings to encourage other teachers to participate and share their experiences. Foster teacher passion by identifying teachers with an interest in gardening or nature, and encouraging them to take a lead role in the garden. Provide opportunities for them to share their knowledge and enthusiasm with colleagues. Support teachers in integrating garden-based activities into their curriculum areas, even if they are not traditionally related to gardening (such as music, art and literature).

Involve parents as partners

Organise working bees at various times, such as weekday evenings and weekend mornings, to accommodate different schedules. Encourage parents to bring their children to working bees, creating a family friendly environment that fosters community spirit. Clearly outline tasks for working bees and allow parents to sign up for specific roles that match their skills and interests. Offer opportunities for parents to contribute from home, such as via grant writing, fundraising or coordinating donations from local businesses. Host regular skills-sharing sessions where parents and community members can share their expertise in gardening, cooking or other relevant areas. Create a supportive environment where parents feel valued for their contributions, regardless of their level of expertise.

Strengthen community connections

Organise community events such as harvest festivals, garden tours or local shows where students can showcase their produce and garden-related projects. Establish partnerships with local businesses, organisations and community groups to support the garden through donations, sponsorships or volunteer efforts. Regularly update the school community about garden activities through social media posts, school newsletters and the school website. Share stories, photos and videos (with appropriate consent) to highlight the garden's impact and encourage community involvement.

*

SEVEN

FAIRY THERAPY

EMOTIONAL TRANSFORMATION IN THE SCHOOL GARDEN

As educators, we often witness the profound impact that school gardens can have on students' lives. These natural spaces serve as fertile ground for personal growth, emotional expression and meaningful connections. In this chapter, we'll explore firsthand accounts of students' experiences in the school garden, highlighting the transformative power of these environments in fostering resilience and relationships.

During a visit to a local school, I had the opportunity to speak with a teacher friend about the school garden. She shared a touching story about a student named Bella, who found solace and joy in the garden's embrace. Bella, who struggled to express her emotions verbally, discovered a sense of calm and purpose while digging in the soil. The sensory activity of gardening allowed her to channel her emotions productively, leading to moments of deep concentration and contentment. Through her connection to the garden, Bella also found a pathway to connect with her teacher and fellow students. The simple act of digging side-by-side with another child became a bridge to friendship, highlighting the transformative power of the school garden in nurturing social bonds and emotional wellbeing.

There are many children like Bella: children who need a distraction or activity to help them create a segue into friendship and connection. The repetitive tasks common in gardening can help them direct energy, frustration, excitement or anxiety into activity. This demonstrates why considering the sociocultural context of the school garden is so important. The 'doing' (Hammel, 2004) aspect of the school garden may be really important for some students as it provides them a pathway into communication with the environment and other people.

Bella had a tendency to pinch when she was frustrated or excited. As her teacher took her into the school garden more often, she noticed that Bella exhibited less of this behaviour and that the garden was having a positive influence on her. Connections with nature, and the connections we have with other people in nature, can have a therapeutic influence on our wellbeing (Ong et al., 2019). I heard many positive stories about children like Bella during my journey of research into school gardens.

Bella's story exemplifies the self-determination that flourishes within school garden environments. By providing open access and free-choice domains, educators empower students to explore and engage with the garden on their terms. Through activities such as digging, planting and nurturing, students like Bella discover their agency and autonomy, paving the way for personal growth and self-expression. All of this helps Bella in her 'becoming' (Hammel, 2004), leading her to become the person that she wants to be, armed with her own agency and a sense of calm confidence to approach life.

Self-regulation in the school garden

Self-regulation is the ability to manage one's emotions, thoughts and behaviours effectively and in different situations. The self-regulation of learning is only one part of a given person's self-regulation (Mujis & Bokhove, 2020). Emphasising the self-regulation of wellbeing is also an important part of enabling children to focus on tasks (and not just learning tasks), develop control over their impulses and adapt to changes and challenges. Self-regulation is multifaceted. It's an integral part of educational settings in that it lays the groundwork for future academic success, social relationships and overall wellbeing (Zimmerman, 2023). Self-regulation is a core aspect of our human functioning that helps facilitate the successful pursuit of personal goals (Inzlicht et al., 2021).

Nature has long been recognised for its calming and restorative effects (Kaplan & Kaplan, 1989; Ulrich, 1993). Several studies have demonstrated that exposure to natural settings can help an individual reduce their stress levels and improve their overall mood and wellbeing, and that this supports efficient and academic cognitive functioning (Berto, 2014; Kuo, 2001). School gardens are one of the only natural environments that children come into contact with regularly, and they provide an ideal environment for fostering self-regulation in young children (Louv, 2008). The sensory experience offered by gardens can help children feel more grounded and focused (Blair, 2009; Williams & Dixon, 2013). School gardens can act as a sanctuary and provide a reprieve from the traditional classroom teaching and learning spaces (although gardens can also be spaces of teaching and learning – which is why their multidimensional meaning and use is so important to understand).

School gardens can also support our use of all eight senses (and yes, there are eight) – visual (sight), auditory (hearing), gustatory (taste), olfactory (smell), tactile (touch), vestibular (balance), proprioception (movement) and interoception (internal).

When I think of the schools I have visited during my career that have used the school garden specifically and deliberately for self-regulation, two examples come to mind. Teacher's aides at both schools would take children into the garden one-on-one when the child signalled or the teacher noticed a need for some self-regulation time. One of these school gardens had a 'calming corner' which was created to support children to process their sensory needs and challenges, and to self-regulate. The calming corner featured some soft grassy spots for lying down or sitting, and children could rub the grass with their palms. There was a slow water feature that was engaging in both sight and sound (and sometimes even touch). The area was also buffered from the rest of the garden, like a cocoon, by fragrant plants and flowers. While this zone was used for specific children who had additional teacher's aides supporting them in the classroom, all children were encouraged to engage with the cocoon of the 'calming corner' during their recreational times if they felt that they needed some self-regulatory time and support.

As a teacher myself, I have witnessed that the school garden significantly improved children's ability to self-soothe and return to classroom activities with a renewed sense of calm. One of my favourite things to do is to use the school garden to facilitate mindfulness activities. I actually love mindful colouring-in, and I would share this with my students. We would work on complex and detailed colouring-in images (often of gardens) for ten minutes each morning in the garden. We'd each take a clipboard and our chosen image (the students would choose from a selection of ten or so) and go into the garden. The students would stretch out, sit up, be on their sides, sit on the bench, sprawl on the grass – whatever was comfortable for them to do their mindful colouring-in. It was such a welcome change from sitting up straight at a desk all day. I always introduced the mindful colouring-in session with a quick meditation: 'What can you hear, feel, see and smell in the school garden today? Is it different to yesterday?' Of course, no one answered out loud – these were internal questions that helped us to understand the concept of interoception (internal sense).

Mindfulness activities further the therapeutic benefits of school gardens. The regular planning or incorporation of these activities into the daily or weekly routine also helps students to see the school garden as a normal part of their everyday lives – and, as we know, regular interactions with nature as children can support our environmental concern as adults (Chawla, 2014). If mindful colouring-in is not your thing, there are many other interactions and activities you can facilitate within the garden as a therapeutic space. Guided meditation, five-minute yoga, creative writing or journalling, reflective sit spots, breathing exercises or simply walking your class through the school garden when transitioning from A to B are all easy ways of incorporating the school garden into your daily teaching practices. Regularly scheduling school garden time, particularly during high-intensity periods (such as the beginning of the school year, end of the school year and evaluation periods) or after high-intensity activities (following recreational periods or physical education classes) can also support children in managing their emotions and behaviours effectively.

School gardens and executive function development

There appears to be an association between self-regulation and executive functioning (Wagner et al., 2020). This is critical to explore, as executive functioning (EF) and self-regulated learning (SRL) are established predictors of academic achievement both current and future (Davis et al., 2021). Understanding how children develop key learning skills can help us, as teachers, parents and the community, to better support their academic journeys.

EF encompasses mental processes such as memory, inhibitory control and cognitive flexibility. These mental processes help children to manage their thoughts, actions and emotions. SRL helps children to navigate their world by setting goals, evaluating their progress towards these goals, and adapting or pivoting to reach the objectives. These skills are strong predictors of academic success both at school and later in life.

In a recent Australian study by Davis et al. (2021), researchers sought to understand the relationship between EF and SRL as children transition from kindergarten to Year 1. The study followed

176 children, starting at the end of kindergarten and following them for the next year. The children's EF was measured through tasks that tested their memory, ability to control impulses and cognitive flexibility. Teachers assessed the children's SRL using a checklist designed to track their independent learning skills. Interestingly, the findings revealed that the EF skills at the end of kindergarten were strong predictors of SRL skills one year later. This means that children who had better memory, impulse control and cognitive flexibility were more likely to excel in setting and achieving learning goals as they moved into Year 1. The findings suggested that while EF significantly influences SRL, they may also be closely related aspects (even though expressed differently) of the same broader cognitive ability. This research highlights the importance of fostering EF in early childhood and early primary schooling as these abilities lay the foundation for successful SRL.

This is why facilitating thought-provoking and engaging activities in school gardens is important. School gardens provide dynamic environments that are continuously evolving. This evolution, along with the unpredictability of nature and the need for continuous adaptation, provides both challenges and opportunities for children to problem-solve and develop critical and flexible thinking. For example, moveable stepping stones can help children reconfigure the layout of the garden to adapt to the seasons; and watering schedules can be adapted to weather patterns to study current watering needs and projections of these needs for the future. Teachers can support the development of EF through structured yet flexible activities in the garden. It is important to integrate core skills such as multi-stage planning and projections, problem-solving, cooperation and collaboration. In this way, school gardens can help children build the skills they need for lifelong learning and achievement.

The school garden can support the development of EF skills via tasks that students set themselves goals for (either consciously or unconsciously). For example, when growing fruits and vegetables, the goal is for the plant to thrive and produce fruit. The student must exercise some EF skills to ensure that they remember to water the plant (memory) and problem-solve any pests that eat the plant (cognitive agility). The goal of producing fruit takes planning, decision-making and adaptability. Cause and effect – which is transferable to many aspects of life – can also be learned through these activities in the school garden.

Witnessing the skills development that occurs in the garden can also help teachers to understand potential barriers and ensure all children can participate, making the garden accessible to all (Taylor et al., 2021). This may mean revising the width of pathways or the height of garden beds for children who have wheelchairs. Sensory pathways might be installed for children who seek sensory fulfilment or calming. A garden with varied types of ground coverings can be soothing – bark, smooth rocks, sand and small pebbles can all provide different feelings underfoot on Barefoot Fridays. Teachers can seek input from their students about their preferences and how they like to interact with and within the school garden. Some students will prefer 'quiet zones' (much like on public transport) that give them a break from the sensory stimulation everywhere in the school environment.

Collaboration with parents is also key. Teachers may wish to ask parents about their children's exposure to nature outside of school through a nature survey – do they live in houses or apartments? Do they have gardens at home? What types of activities does your child like doing in the garden? There are no right or wrong answers. It is just a chance to get to know the level of exposure, needs and challenges of the child in the school garden (and in gardens in their family life). An excellent occasion to share the survey information (while maintaining anonymity) is at a Family Garden Day in which families can come into the garden after school and share their experiences with other families.

Integrating the school garden as a therapeutic space for developing self-regulation and EF offers a more holistic approach to the traditional use and meaning of a school garden in education.

By creating an inclusive, engaging and supportive environment, educators can help children develop these core skills that will help them in their lifelong journey of learning and being. The school garden can be a powerful tool for fostering growth, resilience and a love of learning.

School gardens and self-determination

One school I worked for had a Facebook group for the parents and carers of children within the school community. Most of the posts were from busy working parents who seemed to doubt they were adequately up to date with their busy offsprings' agendas. As a 21st-century parent, it is hard to know who is doing what and when. It often feels like you are failing at everything, and failing everyone, all at once and all the time. I felt the parents' agony as I witnessed explosive comments and very raw moments of stress. I understood the feeling of not only being constantly behind the eight ball, but like the eight ball is on a velodrome and consistently lapping us while crushing and rolling over us in the process.

Some of the comments read:

> 'What time is the Year 4 excursion leaving on Thursday?'
>
> 'My son is telling me it's a free dress day tomorrow and the kids have to wear an orange T-shirt. Is that right? It's 9pm and I don't have an orange T-shirt. He'll have to go in yellow – close enough!'
>
> 'Are there any Year 3 parents who want to pool in for an end-of-year present for Ms K?'

I often just lurked in the shadows since I rarely had the information necessary to respond myself. However, one day a post struck my eye: 'Does anyone have any little fairy statues, jewels or little doors that they would like to donate to the fairy garden project?' asked one mum.

Interested, I quickly clicked on the comments. There were photos and photos of various fairy statues and little coloured stones. A local retiree who enjoyed a little woodwork even made a series of tiny little doors that didn't open to keep all the mysteries inside. What a great idea.

Who said school gardens have to be all fruits and vegetables?

Off the back of this, other parents started to voice their own ideas based on their own interests:

> 'I have a whole lot of dinosaur figurines if you want to make a prehistoric garden!'
>
> 'I have small diggers that could be a quarry or construction site!'
>
> 'I have an old set of wild animals that my children don't use anymore if you would like it!'

After this, the garden went into a rotation of themes – and the best part was, it was completely driven by the parents. The key parent (the one who originally had the fairy garden idea) would pop a box in the office for the donations on a particular theme, called out for via the Facebook group. Parents continued to donate what they had when the call went out. Many parents were happy with this system as they would have just donated the goods to a charity in any case, and this way it was benefiting children that went to school with their own kids (some who might not have the same access to these types of play things). Then, the key parent would get together with some other parents (mostly friends of hers or parents who had children in the same younger grades) to 'design' the fairy garden/prehistoric landscape/quarry/jungle. These parents took photos of themselves decorating the garden and added them to the Facebook group. That way everyone could enjoy in the fun!

I was sceptical at first, I must admit. I thought that these little trinkets would be far too tempting for children to resist pocketing. But, to my surprise, the children didn't take the coloured gems, nor the little Tonka trucks, nor the mighty T-Rex. And I was shocked – I thought for sure things would go walkies. I'm glad that I was proven wrong. Me of little faith.

What this experience demonstrated is that gardens can come in many forms, and that parents are keen for self-determination, too. They want to be able to contribute to the school garden. They want to see their children happy and enjoying the imaginary play that the fairy garden idea inspired.

The benefits of pottering

Within the hubbub of the fairy garden I started to witness small glimmers of quietude. Some children were using the garden as a refuge. It was not to escape – no, it was to embrace! One child embraced her difference, which was that she loved to 'potter'. Pottering means spending your time in a relaxed, leisurely or unhurried way. To potter is to engage in small and often inconsequential tasks or activities. It implies a lack of urgency, where you can move about, seemingly aimlessly (but not always), without a specific goal or deadline. It is a unique way of passing time that encourages peaceful activity.

As a teacher, I would supervise the school garden. I noticed Mei, who visited at lunchtimes. Mei was a potterer. She was a shy child. Mei loved the school garden. She mostly kept to herself and pottered around. Pottering often gets a bad reputation. It's often dismissed as mere dawdling or time-wasting. It's a challenging concept for me, I must admit: I'm quite a busy bee and am not very good at pottering, or mindfulness, or slowing down in any capacity at all really – which is not good, I know, but alas!

In the beginning, I thought that Mei was just meandering (another wonderful word), engaging in seemingly aimless activity. However, over time, I realised that Mei, in her pottering, was being surprisingly productive. She also appeared to be enriching her soul. Through her pottering, Mei seemed to gently disengage from the relentless demands of structured tasks and goals – all quite common in educational settings. The pottering appeared to offer a mental reprieve that fostered her creativity and problem-solving skills. When Mei was pottering around the school garden, she would organise the watering cans (sometimes by colour, sometimes by size, sometimes randomly – although it may not have been random for her), she would tend to the plants, she would stare at the insects and sometimes pick up a tool, only to put it back down a little further away in the garden. This unstructured time in the school garden seemed to act as a creative incubator for Mei. She started to come to me with her musings.

'What language do you think butterflies speak?'

'I don't know. What do you think?'

She thought about it for a minute and went off pottering again. The question remained unanswered. Not all questions need to be answered. It was the pondering and the pottering that was important.

Mei showed me that the ideas that seemed elusive during focused class time would often bubble up to the surface when her mind was allowed to wander in the low-stakes environment of the school garden. It was evident from observing Mei that she found the pottering meditative. Milling around the garden allowed her time for introspection and reflection in ways that a structured meditation or mindfulness session may not – in these quiet moments, Mei connected to herself. She was able to process her thoughts and feelings to gain clarity and peace. Mei was not shy (as I had first thought); Mei was peaceful.

As a peaceful child, Mei's pottering helped her to foster a unique sense of connection to her immediate environment (Chawla, 2014). She engaged with the objects and spaces around her. She sometimes moved a spade or tinkered with a watering can. She would sit on the edge of the above-ground planters or stare up at the scarecrow. By engaging with the objects and spaces, she not only improved her surroundings (by organising the tools, for example) but assisted the development of her own internal landscape – a construction of self.

She had a slow, meandering pace that enabled her to appreciate the small details (such as the ladybug on a leaf that she showed me). You could see her appreciation for the beauties of daily life that the high-speed, goal-oriented educational activities often overlooked.

As Mei's connection to the garden deepened, so too did her sense of pride and accomplishment. Witnessing the fruits of her labour – from the flourishing plants to the newfound friendships or simply side-by-side play, you could see that Mei's interactions instilled a profound sense of satisfaction and joy.

Mei's journey in the garden serves as a reminder of the transformative impact that school gardens can have on students' confidence, resilience and sense of belonging. It provided her with serenity.

I learned a lot from Mei, too. I learned that it is okay to slow down (even while at work). I learned that pottering isn't just about filling time – it is about enriching it. I learned that not all educational experiences have to be structured or planned, and that simply pottering in the school garden creates a foundation for unexpected insights and a refreshed spirit. Mei was right – the best way to grow, sometimes, is by slowing down and giving ourselves the grace to potter.

There are so many holistic benefits of school gardens beyond academic or social achievements. Through experiences in the garden, children can develop essential life skills such as focus, perseverance and empathy, as well as experiencing the right to disengage, have self-preservation and reflect. These skills, nurtured in the garden, equip children (and adults) with the tools they need to navigate challenges and forge meaningful connections both in and out of the classroom.

Messy play in school gardens

Messy play can be incredibly gratifying for some students. It involves activities that celebrate tactile exploration. I once visited a school garden in North Queensland that had a range of different interactive activities. Children could explore different textures – mud, sand, water – and teachers could observe the critical role of messy play in child development. The children loved making mud pies or sandcastles. Not only do children often enjoy it, messy play is also important to their cognitive, emotional and physical growth. Messy play significantly contributes to the development of SRL and EF – both of which have lifelong benefits, as we discussed earlier.

As a teacher, I have always integrated messy play as an integral part of my learning environment. By having messy play, I am encouraging my students to explore their environment and interact with the different textures and substances. These various interactions allow children to further develop their sensory perception and motor skills. Through messy play, children also learn how to appropriately respond to sensory information. I have always found that messy play supports the more complex tasks such as writing, dressing themselves and playing sports.

One of the best things that I have witnessed, as a teacher integrating messy play into my regular teaching, is the development and exhibition of creativity. Some children who are not 'creative' in the traditionally observed outlets (paintings, modelling and so on) can display creative thinking in the garden – that is, thinking outside of the box. The ability to express creativity has, in my own teaching experience, provided students with an opportunity to see themselves as creative and, even more importantly, diverse individuals. Often, children come to believe they are not the 'creative one'; however, humans can be lots of things, and just as the garden is dynamic and changing, so too are we as individuals.

By providing opportunities for messy play in the school garden, teachers can foster a range of benefits that support lifelong success. Embracing messy play in the school garden is imperative to us perceiving both the garden and ourselves holistically and as multidimensional living things. It helps the school garden space and students come to life, and prepares children for their future challenges.

The stories I've shared here are just a few of many examples of the transformative power of school gardens in students', teachers' and parents' lives. By cultivating environments that prioritise self-determination, pride and reflection, educators can empower students to thrive and flourish, both personally and academically. As we continue to nurture school garden programs, let's remain mindful of the profound impact these spaces have on our *being* and our *becoming* through what we are *doing* – or, rather, not doing (Hammel, 2004).

Journal entry seven

How does our garden support emotional transformation?

* How might I encourage imaginary play in our school garden?
* How could I use the school garden to transform challenging behaviours?
* How might I encourage pottering or wandering?
* What are some examples that I have observed of meditation, mindfulness, self-reflection and quietude in our school garden?
* How do these moments of quiet impact development of self?
* What does the development of EF and SRL look like in our school garden?
* What does messy play look like in our school garden?
* What do I observe as the benefits and challenges of messy play?

ACTION PLAN

Encourage imaginary play in the school garden

Create themed areas within the garden, such as fairy gardens, dinosaur landscapes or construction zones, using donated materials from the community. Encourage parents to contribute items and involve students in designing and maintaining these spaces. Organise regular events or storytelling sessions that revolve around the themes in these areas to stimulate students' imaginations and engagement with the garden.

Use the school garden to guide challenging behaviours

Implement activities that channel students' energies and emotions productively, such as digging, planting or other simple repetitive tasks. Designate specific areas or tasks in the garden for students to engage in when they need to self-regulate. Train teachers and support staff to recognise signs of stress or frustration in students and guide them to the garden for calming activities. Use the garden as a space for positive reinforcement, where students can earn time in the garden as a reward for good behaviour or effort.

Encourage pottering and wandering

Allow unstructured time in the garden where students can explore and engage with the environment at their own pace. Create inviting spaces with sensory elements such as fragrant plants, varied textures and quiet corners for reflection. Encourage students to observe and interact with nature, noticing small details and changes over time. Introduce activities that promote mindfulness and reflection, such as nature journalling, drawing or simply sitting quietly and observing the garden.

Foster meditation, mindfulness, self-reflection and quietude

Integrate regular mindfulness activities into the school day, such as guided meditation, yoga or breathing exercises, conducted in the garden. Encourage students to practise mindfulness independently by providing prompts and activities that focus on their senses and surroundings. Create 'quiet zones' in the garden where students can retreat for self-reflection and calm. Use the garden as a transition space between high-intensity activities or classes, allowing students to reset and refocus.

Support the development of EF and SRL skills

Design garden activities that require planning, problem-solving and decision-making, such as planting schedules, pest control or garden design projects. Encourage cooperative tasks where students must work together to achieve a common goal, fostering teamwork and communication. Use the garden as a space to practise goal-setting and progress tracking, with students taking responsibility for specific plants or garden areas. Incorporate garden projects into the curriculum, linking them to subjects such as science, maths and language arts to reinforce academic skills alongside EF and SRL development.

Incorporate messy play into the school garden

Create dedicated messy play areas with materials such as mud, sand, water and natural objects for tactile exploration. Encourage students to engage in activities such as making mud pies, building sandcastles or exploring different textures. Use messy play to support sensory development and motor skills, integrating it into regular garden time. Observe and document the benefits of messy play, such as increased creativity, problem-solving and sensory regulation, and share these observations with parents and the school community.

Engage the community in supporting the school garden

Organise family garden days where parents and students can work together on garden projects, fostering a sense of community and shared responsibility. Utilise social media and school newsletters to communicate about garden activities, successes and needs, encouraging community involvement. Develop partnerships with local businesses, organisations and volunteers to support garden maintenance and development. Provide opportunities for parents and community members to share their skills and knowledge, such as hosting workshops or contributing to themed garden areas.

Evaluate and reflect on garden activities

Regularly assess the impact of garden activities on students' behaviour, emotional wellbeing and academic skills. Gather feedback from students, teachers, parents and community members to understand the benefits and challenges of the garden. Adjust and improve garden programs based on this feedback, ensuring that the garden continues to meet the needs and interests of the school community. Celebrate successes and share stories of transformation and growth within the garden, reinforcing its value as a therapeutic and educational space.

EIGHT

SIR WORMS-A-LOT

SUPPORTING ENVIRONMENTAL SUSTAINABILITY

School gardens are more than just educational tools; they are practical arenas where students can learn about and contribute to environmental sustainability. School gardens can serve as microcosms of larger ecosystems, offering lessons in biodiversity, water management and organic agriculture. It is therefore important that the school garden considers and reflects the local context.

For example, some school gardens incorporate native plants that can help to preserve the local floral and faunal biodiversity, encouraging pollinators such as bees and butterflies to thrive. One school I visited had a shopping mall nearby. The shopping mall had a flat roof which housed non-stinging bees in several hives scattered on it. So when considering the school garden, the local school decided to plant native plants to attract the bees from the roof of the local shopping mall to pollinate the flowers of the fruits and vegetables in their school garden. The planting of local natives and encouraging the nearby bees to the garden was important in this highly urban setting. Without those particular bees or the native plants to attract them, growing fruits and vegetables in this very urban environment would have proven very difficult. This example demonstrates that the success of school gardens in promoting sustainability hinges on context-specific programs that consider the local environment and conditions.

Local context is the cornerstone of school gardens. After all, how good are school gardens for our local children, families, community and environment?

Change for good

Sustainability in education is no longer a choice but a necessity. There is a growing awareness of humans' impact on the planet. And it's funny (#funnynotfunny) that everyone looks to teachers to make a 'change for good', because we are the educators of the people of the future. There are demands for educational systems to drive more sustainable solutions, and yet we don't fully understand the meaning of, or the use that teachers attribute to, school gardens. Solutions need to be comprehensive and fully integrated into the school pedagogy, infrastructure and community connections. But above all else, school gardens must consider and reflect the local context for maximum success.

According to the Australian Education for Sustainability Alliance report *Enablers for Lasting School Change* (2014), there are several critical components to ensure lasting change in schools. Schools implementing and maintaining school gardens need to consider the following to work towards environmental sustainability:

* *Dedicated roles and responsibilities:* Schools must allocate specific roles and responsibilities to staff members to ensure sustainability initiatives are implemented and maintained. This can include sustainability coordinators or green teams.

- *Succession planning:* Sustainable practices should not rely on a single individual. Effective succession planning ensures that sustainability initiatives continue regardless of staff turnover.

- *Constant reinforcement of school philosophy and commitment:* Sustainability must be a core part of the school's philosophy, consistently reinforced through policies, practices and school culture.

- *Accountability:* Schools need clear metrics and accountability measures to track progress and ensure sustainability goals are met.

- *Full community engagement:* Engaging the entire school community, including parents, local businesses and other stakeholders is crucial for the success of sustainability initiatives.

- *Long-term strategic goals:* Sustainability requires a long-term vision with strategic goals that are regularly reviewed and updated.

- *Re-evaluation of how Education for Sustainability (EfS) is embedded in the curriculum:* Schools must continuously assess and refine how sustainability is integrated into teaching and learning.

- *Continuous professional development (PD):* Ongoing PD ensures that educators are equipped with the latest knowledge and skills to teach sustainability effectively.

Both the Australian Curriculum and the Early Years Learning Framework (EYLF) want Australian citizens to develop their eco-literacy – the ability to understand the natural systems that make life on Earth possible. This is a powerful concept that can elevate sustainability education. The EYLF explores sustainability through *Outcome 2: Children are connected with and contribute to their world.* This outcome focuses on supporting children to understand the interconnected relationship with the Earth and how our sustainable practices as humans preserves or impacts that interrelationship.

The Australian Curriculum aims to explore this interdependent and dynamic nature of systems through the diversity of worldviews on ecosystems, values and social justice. It is about building capacity for children to think and act in ways that create a more sustainable future (ACARA, 2023b).

So, what does acting in a way that creates a more sustainable future look like in practice?

Composting

I was once an English language teacher for a class of French eight-year-olds. I would take the children for an hour per day and my role was to speak to them in English. I could teach any subject I wanted, and my heart always pulled towards the sciences. One day I decided that we were going to make mini compost bins in class. We would collect compostable scraps that we would layer into plastic bottles. The bottles needed to be transparent so that we could see the deterioration of each element. The parents must have thought I was mad when I asked them to contribute to the compost project. They were giving their children paper bags of coffee grinds, eggshells and fruit peelings to take to school each day.

The composting process in the school garden enabled students to observe firsthand the importance of using all their scraps (which originally came from the fruits and vegetables grown in the school garden, along with their contributions from home) to fertilise the garden. This project led to the student council setting up a composting bin per class along with creating the role of 'Composting Leader': one child per class who would empty the classroom bin into the larger compost bin in the school garden. It was a student-led project, and the children were able to witness the cycles and the interdependence of the natural world.

The industrial-sized compost bin in the school garden was great for holding the quantity of scraps that the student Composting Leaders were adding from small classroom bins. However, all the magic of composting was now happening in a black opaque bin that we couldn't see the inside of. What was going on? How were the scraps decomposing? Who was doing the decomposing?

I decided we needed to bring the 'Wonder of Worms' into the classroom. I introduced the topic of vermiculture – which is simply composting by worms. We observed the worms through a transparent container and could witness them breaking down the organic matter. Of course, we couldn't give all the scraps to the worms – otherwise, we would have had worms the size of Godzilla – but I did select about one student per week to give their decent-sized scrap stash to the worms. The children could now witness how the worms ate and digested the food scraps, turning them into fertile, rich compost. Once the scraps were composted, the students would tip the contents into the school garden beds and we would start over again.

The 'Wonder of Worms' project taught the students several skills. One that I appreciated the most was the leadership skills I saw developing. The students had to be responsible and take care of the worms. They also had to be careful when transporting the compost to the garden to use on the garden beds and ensure that the worms were safe and unharmed (not to mention being responsible for their own personal hygiene around the worm activity). This experiential learning experience made science come alive for the children, and many developed a deeper appreciation and care for the worms. Some students even game them names; at one stage, we had Wormsworth, Bendy Benny and Nibbles!

Water conservation

Think of your teaching experiences. Even within the first few years of teaching you may have experienced a rural setting, a regional setting, a coastal setting or an urban setting. These settings offer unique environmental opportunities and challenges.

One of the schools that I worked in was in an area in which it rained a lot (like, a *lot*). Another was in an area in which it rained very little.

In the school where it rained very little, it was important for the school garden to demonstrate agility in the way that water was used and conserved. There are several ways in which water conservation can occur in a school garden.

One school that I visited had a cistern to collect and store rainwater from the adjacent classroom buildings. The cistern had a transparent panel which was used for learning. Students would record the water levels within the cistern, statistically tracking how much water was being collected and how much water was evaporating at any one point in time. The tracking data was made available to the public via the school Facebook page, and the 'rain watch' even became a point of conversation at children's birthday parties. Parents shared that this was a welcome change in conversation, as environmental perspectives were something of a taboo for this community. It provided parents with a talking point as a jump zone to launch into other environmentally minded conversations with their peers.

At another school I visited with very little rainfall, school garden maintenance was challenging because it takes quite a lot of water to maintain a garden. Paying for the quantity of water that the garden needed was a big challenge for the leadership team, which caused them to question whether the school garden was worth the cost. Then, in a last-ditch attempt to save the garden, the leadership team thought of a different solution. The groundskeeper suggested that the grass clippings from the ride-on mower could be used as a form of insulating mulch on the garden beds. By repurposing the grass clippings, the little water that did fall was able to be 'captured' in the ground and protected from evaporation by the grass clippings. Sometimes the best solutions can come from people who are peripheral to the teaching staff, so it is always good to ask who in the school community might have the skills or knowledge to help with the task or challenge.

The fact that assistance may come from the most unlikely places is why considering the local context when designing and implementing school gardens is so important. One of the schools that I visited was located in a semi-arid region, so water conservation was a principal concern for the plants in the school garden. The garden had not flourished in the past partly because the plants that were included were not suited to the climate, and ended up dying. At this school, we proposed the 'problem' to the students and asked them to work in small groups to workshop possible solutions. These types of real-world problem-solving activities support children to develop transferable skills such as critical thinking, collaboration and innovation.

One group came up with the idea of a drip irrigation system. They proposed the activity would help them to establish some engineering skills to measure and understand the terrain and possibly some of the inclines that they would have to navigate. They proposed to first measure the water usage of the garden in its current state and then measure the usage of water with the drip system and see if it made a difference (and how significant that difference might be). They then suggested that they transform the value in litres to a dollar value, calculating how much money the school could save over a year. I tested their critical thinking by saying, 'Yes, but the system costs money to establish.' The students responded that they would take those costs out of the first year's margin of savings from transferring to the drip method, and would project a further five years of the drip method to justify that the overall savings far outweighed the initial installation costs. It was simply brilliant!

Later, after the drip irrigation system had been installed (with a few challenges), another group of students wanted to redesign the whole garden to minimise water use. They suggested that the challenges of the drip system could be due to the existing inclines and declines within the garden. Their solution to this was to completely rethink the garden layout. I was surprised that one of the students, Ali, knew the actual name for this concept – xeriscaping. I had to admit that I had never heard that word before and I asked him how he knew it. He said that his dad often spoke about xeriscaping as it was part of his business. Ali's family had moved from Yemen and his father was a landscape architect, so his dad often sat with him, showed him his drawings and talked about water-saving techniques he picked up from his work in Yemen that he could now use in Australia. I watched as Ali excitedly told his classmates about some of the techniques he knew: 'We could only water at night-time; or plant hardy plants; or create mountains or moats to direct the water to the plants!' He had some good ideas about the use of pebbles and bark to 'trap' the water in the soil. But most of all, I loved his excitement and the way he shared his enthusiasm with his friends. Ali was always quite quiet in the classroom – he had moved at eight years old and was still catching up with the language and the cultural ways of education in Australia. But in this moment, he was the knowledge holder – he had the information, and being in the garden provided him an opportunity to feel good about himself.

Native planting

One of the important aspects of school gardens is that people feel that their identities and the identities of their communities are represented in the space. The grapevine example I discussed in chapter 3 is an example of how climate-appropriate plants can be integrated into school gardens, both to ensure suitability for growing in that space and to reflect the sociocultural identity of the school community. Native plants can be used in school community celebrations to honour the cultural groups within the school, or recognise important religious, cultural, historical or national commemorations, celebrations or pastimes. In this way, the use of native plants in the school garden can fortify both school and community togetherness.

One school I visited had dedicated sections of the garden to the diverse cultural groups within the school community. Families were invited to provide seeds or seedlings for plants that represented their cultural heritage. This is obviously a very subjective activity and there were some very interesting interpretations, driven by what the families felt identified with their cultural heritage the most. One North American family donated corn seedlings. The type of corn they provided was perfect for popping. The students tended to the corn, watched and measured its growth, harvested it and dried it. Finally, the day came to test whether the corn would pop. Would it pop? Would it? It did! Hoorah! The kids just loved it – so many excited faces. There was corn everywhere!

Another family brought in a lot of herbs. They planted herbs that they used in their traditional cuisine – mint, parsley and a bay tree were all part of the garden. We had a Herb Harvest Festival and used all the herbs from the garden to make tabbouleh.

Another time, one of the parents came to the school and gave a talk in the school garden about Eid al-Fitr. It was very interesting for the non-Muslim children at the school to learn about another faith. Everyone was able to establish a greater understanding of one another through joy, gratitude and community for all students, all taking place in the school garden.

Organic and pollinator gardens

Organic gardening is an interesting lens through which to talk about the state of our planet. Students and teachers can discuss what it means to avoid the use of pesticides in gardening, and what benefits and challenges this can present.

One school I visited that gardened organically faced an infestation of slugs and snails. Snails were eating all of the lettuce leaves and it was very difficult to get even one small lettuce to optimum growth. The teacher who was in charge of the garden asked the students to form small groups and problem-solve together. The issue was presented in a fun and dynamic manner – 'The case of the eaten lettuce leaves' – and the children had to work together, using critical thinking, to solve the problem.

The teacher shared that the students came up with many different solutions. The first was to put beer in an empty bottle to drown them. This was discounted because a) the use of beer at school was inappropriate, and b) because snails and slugs drowning in the beer is inhumane and certainly not appropriate for a school environment. (I can only imagine the letter the teacher would receive if little Johnny had gone home and told his parents that he spent his day at school drowning slugs and snails in beer in the school garden.) Thankfully there were other solutions, too. One group suggested that they place ash around the lettuces so that the perpetrators could not get to it; another group thought a natural spray (maybe peppermint leaves in water?) might work; and another suggested that the lettuce be planted in raised garden beds (and that maybe the sides would be too long for tempted snails and slugs to climb).

This opportunity to problem-solve a real-life issue within an educational context creates a foundation for children to develop and implement skills in a familiar and scaffolded environment, which adequately prepares them for challenges and opportunities they may experience in their life after or outside of school. Additionally, working in small groups provides children with an opportunity to develop their 21st-century skills, notably cooperation and collaboration – working with their classmates, listening to each other, presenting and considering ideas. All these skills are valuable and transferable to other environments and truly helps them to develop as citizens.

Another aspect of organic gardening is pollinator gardens. A specialist pollinator garden can attract butterflies and bees, which can provide a sense of wonderment for children and a level of serenity in the school garden, along with organic pest control. Children can develop their curiosity through the observation of pollinators and the process of pollination and predation, increasing their knowledge and understanding of life cycles and the interconnectedness of beings. Not only this, but by encouraging pollinators to the school garden, the vegetables, fruits and flowers have optimum potential.

Vertical gardening

Vertical gardens come in all different varieties. In one of the colder climates that I visited, a school had a vertical garden that was a flat wall of succulent plants. The different variations of green and purple were visually pleasing, particularly against the nuances of grey that filled in the skyline. In another school, the vertical garden consisted of old pipes that a parent (who was a plumber) had donated to the school. They were mostly off-cuts of pipes that he had fit at work – so he had a lot of odds and ends left over, and as the pipes would have ended up in landfill it was a sustainable option to repurpose them. The pipes were sawn in half horizontally and planted with strawberry plants. The red strawberries hung over the edge of the pipes, glistening in the sunlight. There were designated times in which the children were allowed to 'sample' some of the ripe strawberries. Nothing can replace the smile of a child who has waited and waited for a strawberry to go from green to white to red before eating it. It is just magic.

The complexities of the natural world

Now, the natural world provides opportunities, but it also provides challenges. One of the school gardens that I worked in was a walled garden in an inner-city urban school. I took great lengths to ward off 'pests' – but as an environmentally conscious person, I did not want to cause harm or use any toxic products within the garden. Both for the children and the animals' sake.

One day, I took the children to do an Easter egg hunt in the garden. I had hidden all the eggs after school the day prior and, as the garden was within the gated walls of the school complex, I was convinced that the chocolate eggs would be all right and ready for the hunt the next morning. As I arrived with my class of children, I could see the metallic wrappings glistening in the sun. Hoorah! The eggs were still there and the plan had worked. I was excited and triumphant. There were gleeful smiles as we descended the ramp into the garden. Just then, as if straight out of a horror film, I saw a neatly decapitated rabbit, body and head cleanly apart, right near the first Easter eggs at the end of the ramp. As if it were a welcoming present to my class of five-year-olds. Happy Easter – here is a decapitated bunny. Of course, I quickly turned on the children (with an excited, not alarmed, face) and announced that the Easter bunny actually left the eggs in the classroom and that I was just playing a joke on them. We went back into the classroom (with no one seeing the bunny – thank goodness) and I immediately rang the maintenance person.

'We have a dead bunny,' I announced.

He was stunned and silent for a moment before retorting in his thick Irish accent, 'Well, what do you want me to do about it then?'

I actually didn't know. I wasn't on morning tea duties that day, so I asked him to come down to the school garden then and we'd see about it together. So there we stood. I had on hot pink tights to match the joyful Easter theme and he had a four-leafed clover tattoo on his ankle. And at that ankle height was the lifeless decapitated bunny.

But it didn't make sense. Why was the bunny decapitated? Who would have done this? We took the bunny's body away and chalked it up to an isolated incident. Weeks passed and all was well in the school garden. Until there was a second decapitated bunny. Clean off. Done with precision. I reported it to the town hall – it was a walled garden, so someone was obviously getting in at night or throwing the corpse over the outside walls into the children's garden. Maybe as a sick joke? Maybe it was kids, as a prank? Whatever it was, it was increasing in frequency. By now five bunnies had made it into the garden – always in two pieces, always with the same sharp precision. I spoke to the mayor again. He said because of the frequency, the population of children who used the garden and that these events were occurring at night-time, it merited going to the police. So, there I was, a teacher sitting in a police station talking about decapitated rabbits in the school garden. The police officer agreed that this appeared to be human activity as the rabbits were sizable and the cut lines so clean. They set up a nocturnal camera on the garden to catch the villain.

Low and behold! On the fifth night, the camera captured a rabbit hopping around the school garden. It was nibbling at the lettuce leaves. Innocent enough – we had to let nature live as intended, so the rabbit having a little snack was not a bother until… slinking on top of the wall was a dark silhouette. It was big. It waited. The rabbit kept nibbling at the lettuce unaware of the danger lurking just above it. Then, swoosh – just one jump! The predator jumped off the wall, pulled the rabbit's head back with one claw and decapitated it with the other. Strangely, almost immediately, it exited – jumped back over the wall and into the darkness.

We had to let the local community know of the predators lurking in the night. I sent a letter to local residents:

> *Dear Residents,*
>
> *Could you please keep your cats inside at night-time?*
> *One is decapitating rabbits in the school garden.*
>
> *Sincerely,*
>
> *Emma Derainne*
> *Teacher*

Be a teacher, they said. It'll be fun, they said.

This story demonstrates that we can sometimes have unusual and unexpected issues related to our local context that we may encounter in the school garden. Not all school gardens will have cats that decapitate rabbits; nonetheless, the local context requires critical consideration in the planning, implementation and maintenance of school gardens. We must be aware of the challenges and opportunities of our unique surroundings.

Journal entry eight

How does our garden support environmental sustainability?

- How familiar am I with the key documents and policies of Education for Sustainability (EfS)?
- In what ways can we align our school's curriculum and objectives with the principles outlined in these publications?
- How can I incorporate eco-literacy into my teaching practices?
- What strategies can I use to help children connect with and contribute to their world?
- How does our school garden contribute to environmental sustainability?
- What practical sustainability activities do we integrate into our school garden?
- What native plants could I suggest for our school garden?
- What unexpected challenges have we faced in maintaining the school garden and how might we address these challenges?
- What strategies have we employed to make the garden thrive in an urban environment?
- How do we ensure the safety of our students while they are working in the garden? What measures do we take to address potential hazards, such as pests or harmful plants in the garden?

ACTION PLAN

Ensure familiarity with key Education for Sustainability (EfS) documents and policies

Begin by ensuring all staff are familiar with the Australian Curriculum and Early Years Learning Framework regarding EfS. Schedule PD sessions to review key documents and discuss how they align with your school's objectives. Provide access to resources and encourage ongoing learning and discussion about these principles among staff.

Align curriculum with sustainability principles

Review your school's curriculum to identify areas where sustainability principles can be integrated. Work with teachers to embed these principles into lesson plans, projects and everyday classroom activities. Develop specific units or projects that focus on sustainability topics, such as composting, water conservation and native planting.

Incorporate eco-literacy into teaching practices

Encourage teachers to incorporate eco-literacy into their teaching practices by integrating lessons about natural systems, biodiversity and sustainability into various subjects. Use the school garden as a hands-on learning environment where students can observe and interact with these concepts. Develop activities and projects that emphasise the interconnectedness of natural systems and human impact on the environment.

Connect students with their world

Foster a sense of connection and responsibility among students by involving them in the planning, maintenance and use of the school garden. Encourage them to explore their local environment and understand their role in preserving it. Organise field trips, guest speakers and community projects that highlight local environmental issues and solutions.

Contribute to environmental sustainability

Ensure that the school garden is designed and maintained with sustainability in mind. Use organic gardening methods, composting, water-conservation techniques and native plants to create a sustainable and educational environment. Regularly evaluate and update garden practices to ensure they align with sustainability goals.

Incorporate practical sustainability activities

Incorporate a variety of sustainability activities into the school garden program. Establish composting systems and teach students about the decomposition process and nutrient cycling. Implement water-saving techniques, such as rainwater harvesting and drip irrigation. Engage students in planting and caring for native plants to promote local biodiversity.

Plant native plants in the school garden

Research and select native plants that are well-suited to your local environment. Involve students in the process by having them research and propose plants that could be included in the garden. Create themed garden areas that represent different aspects of local flora and cultural heritage.

Address unexpected challenges

Prepare for unexpected challenges by developing a flexible and adaptive approach to garden management. Encourage open communication among staff, students and the community to identify and address issues as they arise. Document challenges and solutions to build a knowledge base for future reference.

Implement strategies for urban environments

Implement strategies to make the garden thrive in an urban environment, such as vertical gardening, container gardening and utilising small spaces efficiently. Collaborate with local businesses and organisations to secure resources and support for the garden. Engage the community in garden projects and events to foster a sense of ownership and investment.

Ensure safety in the garden

Develop and enforce safety protocols for students working in the garden. Provide proper training on the safe use of tools and equipment. Conduct regular safety inspections to identify and address potential hazards, such as pests or harmful plants. Ensure that students are supervised at all times and educate them on how to recognise and avoid potential dangers.

NINE

ROOTS OF CONNECTION

THE HOLISTIC BENEFITS OF SCHOOL GARDENS

While the common narrative often highlights the health and nutritional benefits of school gardens, their potential extends far beyond these aspects. This chapter delves into the multifaceted advantages of school gardens, revealing how they serve as powerful tools for fostering community connection, cultural heritage and overall student development. Throughout this chapter, I explore the diverse ways school gardens contribute to educational and social environments, providing practical guidance for integrating these insights into your own school garden initiatives.

Towards the end of the chapter, you'll find a step-by-step guide to help you implement or enhance a school garden, ensuring that it becomes an integral part of your school's culture and curriculum. By embracing the broader benefits of school gardens, we can create inclusive and enriching spaces that support the holistic development of students, foster community engagement and celebrate cultural diversity.

Community connection and cultural heritage

School gardens are powerful catalysts for community engagement and neighbourhood revitalisation. My exploration into school gardens revealed that teachers consistently emphasised the importance of community involvement in the school garden, which often included parents, community members and the students themselves. These gardens serve as focal points for fostering connections within the school community and beyond, contributing to a sense of belonging and community cohesion (Hammel, 2004).

Connection was a prominent theme across all of the schools that I visited, yet it manifested differently within each sociocultural context. One of the primary schools I visited is located in an area that was previously an agricultural settlement. The original station property, bordered by a state forest, was subdivided to create the township in the late 1800s, resulting in properties within the township being quite close together. Within the sociocultural context of this rural primary school, the strong agricultural traditions of the community were seen as a way to connect students with their community's heritage, teach practical skills related to farming and gardening, and instil a sense of pride in the local identity.

The principal of the school shared the 'big-hearted community nature' of his school. However, simultaneously, this school decided to integrate a Yarning Circle into their school garden, reflective of the many Aboriginal students within the school community. First Nations families drove the design, consultation and implementation of the Yarning Circle within an educational setting that had been traditionally void of Aboriginal and Torres Strait Islander perspectives, and historically ingrained with colonialist views due to the settlement history of the area (Oulton

& Jagger, 2023). In contemporary times, this rural primary school placed value on the cultural diversity of its school community through their school garden. This notion of the garden as a positive space for building relationships aligns with previous research that highlights the role of gardens in strengthening communities and generating social capital (Lucke et al., 2019; Fieldhouse, 2003; Firth et al., 2011; Teig et al., 2009; Whatley et al., 2015; Veen et al., 2016).

This rural primary school serves as an example of how students can thrive through the meaning, values, knowledge and activities of a school garden designed with all students' cultural perspectives in mind. The newly renovated garden at this school aligns with the priorities, values and sociocultural capital of the school community, demonstrating how rural and Aboriginal traditions can significantly influence the direction of school garden initiatives. This school adopted a 'wrap-around' curriculum approach, prioritising the garden for students by dedicating Friday afternoons to gardening activities. It was a time when the community was invited in to share knowledge and skills, do activities (singing, art, music) or just 'be' in the garden. I witnessed many interesting inter-age and cross-cultural conversations within this school's garden. The garden was not just a *place* but a *space* – living, dynamic and ever-evolving.

Therapeutic benefits and emotional wellbeing

I've discussed extensively in this book that school gardens can be excellent spaces to support mental health and emotional wellbeing, particularly in challenging sociocultural contexts. Teachers have acknowledged the positive impact of school gardens on student wellbeing and development. Gardens provide therapeutic spaces, sensory experiences and opportunities for skill development. Students take pride in their gardening projects, find joy in watching their plants and produce grow, and benefit from peer-to-peer connections facilitated by the gardens. Teachers have communicated the therapeutic and calming influence of the school garden on their students, especially those with specific sensory needs or as a tool to guide challenging behaviours. The physical activity of gardening is also beneficial (Ahmed et al., 2011), particularly for students with special needs, offering a feeling of sensory fulfilment.

It is important, however, that there are appropriate safety and security measures in place to ensure that school gardens are welcoming and accessible for all students. Ong et al. (2019) revealed that participants attributed meaning to community gardens through their therapeutic aspects and that this can be facilitated through safe spaces. The school garden offers sensory activities that encourage its use as a therapeutic space, showing that school gardens are not only welcoming but necessary for children to support mental and emotional health.

Skills development and social connections

During my research, teachers highlighted the development of skills within the school garden. These aimed to teach life skills for improved autonomy. Teachers also stated that skill development gave students opportunities to learn competencies that might be useful in future employment. Teaching students how to grow their own food and cook for themselves from a sustainability perspective, influenced by the school's agricultural heritage, was a positive step towards autonomy and self-sufficiency for some communities. The theme of skills development aligns with previous research claiming that school gardens teach students about sustainable agricultural practices and instil a sense of responsibility towards the environment (Blair, 2009). Teachers felt that this helped students feel empowered, echoing research by Bowker and Tearle (2007) that experiential learning in natural settings helps students construct new knowledge, skills and values.

Friendship-building is another skill fostered in the school garden. Teachers attributed meaning to the garden through its ability to connect peers, providing a safe space to build one-on-one friendships and develop social skills. Additionally, the teacher-student connection is strengthened in the school garden, particularly for students who struggle to have conversations in traditional educational environments. Teachers conveyed that students were more likely to interact with their peers in the garden, aligning with findings that natural settings foster social interactions for children (Chawla et al., 2014; Henryks, 2011; Block et al., 2012; Cutter-Mackenzie, 2009).

Connection to environmental education

In regions with a strong environmental consciousness, teachers may view the school garden as an opportunity to share their personal interests and passion for gardening, nature and outdoor activities. This intrinsic motivation drives their involvement and investment in the garden, contributing to its success and sustainability. Parents and teachers can also share their advocacy for sustainability. At one school I visited, the garden was initially established by parents who advocated for its installation. Teachers quickly echoed the sentiment, forming a small group of volunteer teachers for recreational supervision duties, which contributed to the garden's success. Teachers and parents at this urban school seemed to understand that opportunities for children to connect with nature are diminishing (Louv, 2009). They recognised that school gardens offer numerous health and wellbeing benefits (Chawla et al., 2014; Wei, 2012). Due to the urban context of the school, the garden was viewed as one of the few avenues for teaching students about sustainability, biodiversity and conservation.

School gardens and literacy

School gardens are a great place to learn literacy skills. One particular school (which had a strong focus on dictation) I visited would take the children to the school garden to write and rewrite their words of the week. Sometimes the words were in some way related to the garden, but other weeks they were not – and the garden was simply treated as a creative environment to support the reflection, execution and memorisation of certain words. Now, not all educational contexts operate in this manner (nor should they, necessarily), however, for this particular environment that placed a strong emphasis on dictation, completing this exercise in the school garden provided at least a glimmer of 'extraordinary' for a task that could have been perceived as military.

Children were also responsible for writing the signage in the school garden. Each time there was a school celebration, the garden would come alive with stories, messages, poems, chants, reports and historical accounts inspired by the students', teachers', families' and community members' interactions with and within the school garden. There were literacy benches that had a small 'book borrowing' house on a raised pole. Children could open the door of the waterproof book house and select a book that they could read while sitting on the literacy bench in the garden. As this reading experience was outside, some children much preferred it to going to the library, even though there were fewer books to choose from – it was the ability to sit in the sun and enjoy the book that the students seemed to appreciate. The school garden became a real literacy space, where creativity, imagination and storytelling came to life. Book borrowing and book benches are a fantastic way of encouraging literacy in the school garden.

More than just gardens

School gardens extend far beyond providing only health and wellbeing benefits. While these health and wellbeing aspects are positive, school gardens are multifaceted spaces that support children's holistic development in diverse and profound ways. Drawing on Hammel's (2004) framework of doing, being, belonging and becoming, this book has explored how school gardens can foster critical 21st-century skills such as cooperation, collaboration, critical thinking, wonderment and curiosity.

This comprehensive analysis has delved into the intricate relationship between sociocultural contexts and the meanings that educators attribute to school gardens. It is evident that school gardens are adaptable, reflecting the unique needs, values and goals of their local communities. They serve as hubs for environmental education, community involvement and the cultivation of a sense of responsibility towards nature. These gardens reconnect children with the natural world, instilling a sense of stewardship and a lifelong appreciation for the environment.

School gardens also play a crucial role in promoting community cohesion. They provide spaces for collaborative activities that strengthen community ties and celebrate local heritage and traditions. These gardens can be inclusive environments that cater to the diverse needs of all students, including those with special educational requirements. By offering sensory experiences and fostering a sense of belonging, school gardens contribute to children's personal and social development.

The significance of customising school garden initiatives to suit the sociocultural contexts of each school is paramount. Flexible and adaptive programs that resonate deeply with community values, traditions and aspirations are essential for the success and sustainability of school gardens. This book has highlighted the importance of integrating sociocultural contexts into the analysis and design of school garden programs, ensuring that they are inclusive and contextually relevant.

Future directions

To maximise the potential of school gardens, it is essential to address barriers and provide teachers with the necessary resources and training. By doing so, we can ensure that school gardens are not only established but also effectively utilised to support the development of vital skills in children. This preparation will enable our students to grow into environmentally conscious and capable decision-makers in the future. Ensuring that children have access to, and actively engage with, school gardens can significantly impact their ability to develop cooperation, collaboration, critical thinking, wonderment and curiosity – skills that are essential for their personal growth and our planet's wellbeing.

Next steps – the practical plan for your school garden

As a teacher inspired by the varied roles and benefits of school gardens discussed in this book, you may now be considering how to start or enhance a school garden at your own school. Here's a step-by-step plan to guide you through the process. Flip to the back of the book for a handy summary of each step.

STEP 1: Initial planning and assessment

Start by assessing the current situation of your school garden. Identify any gaps that might exist by asking the following questions:

- [ ] Are there any existing garden spaces or do we have to create one?
- [ ] Do we have the available tools to be able to create or renovate an existing garden space?
- [ ] What does the existing or proposed space look like? Will we have in-ground or raised beds? Will there be an orchard or not?
- [ ] What is the current condition of the resources that we have at hand (tools, garden beds and so on)?
- [ ] Who are our potential stakeholders?
- [ ] How do students attribute meaning to the school garden?
- [ ] How do parents attribute meaning to the school garden?
- [ ] How do other teachers attribute meaning to the school garden?

- [ ] How do school administrators attribute meaning to the school garden?
- [ ] How do community members attribute meaning to the school garden?

Set goals and objectives:

- [ ] What is the purpose of our school garden?
- [ ] What is it that we hope to achieve with the garden?
- [ ] How can we use the school garden for educational purposes?
- [ ] How can we use the school garden for community-building?
- [ ] How can we use the school garden for promoting sustainability?
- [ ] How can we ensure that the school garden becomes a therapeutic and inclusive space?

Now, set yourself clear objectives using the SMART framework to ensure the success and sustainability of your school garden project. SMART goals are specific, measurable, achievable, relevant and time-bound. For example, to set a specific goal, you might ask the question:

What is it that I want to accomplish?

Example response:

I want to increase the number of children who use the garden.

Set specific steps to provide depth to this specific goal. This can be executed by identifying how your own personal goal for the school garden aligns with the broader vision or values of the school and/or wider community. You might also add some information about how you might achieve this goal. An example may be to specify that you want to increase student participation through experiential learning activities that promote environmental stewardship.

It is also integral to define the scope of the goal. It can be challenging to attempt to implement or renovate the entire garden at once. Instead, aim for specific areas or aspects of the school garden project that you want to address, prioritise these areas and work through them one by one. You might only have a small, very targeted goal; for example: *Increase student participation at the after-school garden club*. Whatever the size of the goal, at least you are getting started!

STEP 2: Engage the community and gather support

We all need support. Think about who you can reach out to. Some people have more time than others, and sometimes we need to request support from a little further afield to get things moving.

How might other teachers offer their support? We know that teachers are time poor, so think more creatively about how colleagues might 'support' the garden – lunch duty supervision, contributing to an ideas board or creating social media posts are all ways to support the school garden without ever touching any soil or devoting hours to the cause.

Who might be your champions? Are there community members (with current, valid Working with Children Checks and who have jumped over all the red tape) who might be able to come into the school? Even if those people don't have Blue Cards, for example, can they contribute from the comfort of their own home? I know many Baby Boomers who are more connected to their devices than adolescents (although they'd rarely admit it).

You'll need the school administrators on board, too. The importance of this may not be evident at first; but if you want to organise a box to collect fairy statues, the school administrator is the person to do it – so you need them on your side.

How do parents perceive and experience the school garden? Do they value it and, if so, how? You may find that parents are hesitant to be involved (this was my own experience). This is because many come from elsewhere, don't want to step on toes, aren't sure about the 'norms' and might not have the time (among other things). So, you have to really think about how you want to approach your parents. If you go in there asking for volunteers on a regular basis, you may find that people generally don't want to regularly give up their time for free or be locked into a volunteer position. However, if you find a way to pitch the garden group as the 'in' thing, people might just get on board. One school that I visited had a group of parents that called themselves the 'Gardening Gurus'. The group comprised five or so parents who would hang out in the garden. Sometimes they would garden, sometimes they would just be together and chat (one of the key reasons of having a garden is to connect with one another, after all). They would run the after-school garden club once a month and would have seasonal festivals in the garden. It was rough-and-tumble, an organised chaos, but it looked like fun and people wanted to join them. So, they started having working bees, where people could start to test their skills in the garden. The Gurus were welcoming and, above all, had no agenda – you came as you were. There was a rather simple 'don't be a dick' philosophy that promoted harmony and happiness.

As you will have seen in this book, there are many diverse roles that people can occupy to support the garden in one way or another. People will generally work harder at things they enjoy – so encourage participants to self-elect into the various roles and responsibilities: project manager, fundraiser, garden coordinator and communication lead are all positions that will help implement and maintain a thriving and successful school garden.

Just as the Garden Gurus did, you can host community meetings. At these meetings, you can share your collective ideas and visions for the school garden. Listen to others' views and appreciate the community's concern to ensure that the garden is achieving the needs and expectations of the people it serves (and that serve it). These community meetings, festivals and celebrations build enthusiasm for the school garden and serve as a platform for encouraging community involvement. People will want to feel a part of something if they intrinsically value it. Gather some gurus around you.

STEP 3: Design the garden

First, you will need to conduct a site analysis. This may seem unnecessary, but it is one of the most integral parts of setting up a school garden. Conducting a site analysis is critical in understanding the unique challenges and opportunities of a school garden.

At one school I visited, the school garden, situated on the back perimeter near a coastal path and sand dunes, had been in place since the school's establishment. This location, while picturesque, had led to the presence of tiger snakes, a common hazard in the area. The garden featured raised beds with wide alleys to ensure wheelchair accessibility, primarily cultivating herbs and citrus trees, but also contained substantial portions that were unused and overgrown. The entire school was fenced, and an additional interior fence was added around the garden in 2022 for safety and security, addressing concerns around student protection from potential wildlife threats and ensuring they remained within a safe area. Teachers had the key to the garden, allowing access as needed, and the garden was predominantly used during recreational times. The proximity of the garden to the coastline and the associated risks of snake sightings necessitated thorough planning and regular site analysis to maintain a secure and beneficial environment for the students.

So, while an initial site analysis may seem mundane, it can mean the difference between a snake bite (or not)! And, as a teacher, you certainly don't want to have to explain to Charmaine's parents how she got bitten by a tiger snake at school and was rushed to hospital. But don't let snakes deter you. It takes a little more careful planning but the school garden experience can still be wonderful – snakes (hopefully only peripherally) and all!

Another important concern is the soil quality of the school garden. One of my teacher friends did not apologise for her lack of interest in engaging with her school garden. She stated that she didn't want to go through all the administrative red tape and that by the time she had done all that (on the rare occasions she did go through the process), she had lost all energy and enthusiasm for the garden experience. This is a common feeling among teachers, particularly in Australia where the amount of red tape is a lot more challenging than what I had witnessed teaching overseas. However, it is important to test the soil quality as poor soil quality can have detrimental effects on both plant and human health. There are some soil-borne diseases and it is important to ensure that you are taking the correct hygiene and safety precautions to protect you and your students. Therefore, when you are evaluating the site, assess the soil quality, sunlight exposure, water availability and space constraints to ensure that you have maximum chances at success for your school garden.

To simplify the process and maintain enthusiasm for the garden, consider several practical approaches. One option is to seek out local universities that offer soil-testing services. For instance, Macquarie University in Sydney provides soil testing for harmful chemicals, which can help ensure the safety and health of the garden environment. Utilising such services can alleviate the burden on teachers by outsourcing the technical aspects of soil-quality assessment to professionals.

A more hands-on approach can be both educational and manageable. DIY pH testing kits are widely available and can be used to assess the soil's acidity or alkalinity. This activity not only serves a practical purpose but also offers a valuable learning experience for students. By involving students in testing and analysing soil samples, teachers can integrate science lessons directly into the gardening experience, fostering a deeper connection and understanding of the natural world.

In the analysis consider safety and security. This is important for children from the outside environment, but also sometimes children from one another if some of the children are prone to throwing objects or escaping. One of the key reasons for having a fence around the school garden (in addition to the school perimeter fence) is that it prevents unauthorised access. By restricting access to the garden, the fence keeps people out at times when the garden is fragile (providing the garden some time to grow and flourish) and protecting the children within the garden from being distracted by other visitors to the school. The fence around the school garden also prevents unwanted wildlife from entering the garden. In Australia, some wildlife can be pests to school gardens – including snakes, toads and possums. One school I visited had a big issue with fruit bats eating all the fruit from the orchard. The bats would take one bite out of many of the hanging fruit, but left the rest on the tree, which meant that it had to be removed by teachers so that children wouldn't eat the fruit (not knowing that a bat had bitten it). Fences also play a role in protecting the children. With a fence around the school garden, teachers and parents are able to let students wander around the garden without the risk of running off and encountering external dangers.

It is important to have an understanding of who can access the garden and when. This typically involves addressing several questions, including who will have the key for the school garden, and when the school garden will be open for use. Clear scheduling prevents conflicts and ensures that the garden is available for its intended purposes. Allocating specific times to different classes may be one option to help manage the space; however, it is also beneficial to have inter-age slots so that siblings can play together in the garden, or children can meet other students from other age groups.

One suggestion for managing the inter-age access of the school garden, but maintaining age-specific activities, is to designate class-level spaces. These spaces may rotate on a term-by-term basis and could include a sensory space, a vegetable plot and an insect or native garden space. I personally love to observe how students interact with these spaces organically. Through this, you will start to understand what meaning students attribute to their school garden space.

Start designing the layout of the garden. Designing a school or kitchen garden is part of the Year 5 and 6 Technologies Curriculum.

You may want to run this activity with the upper primary students and get them to use their critical thinking skills to analyse the space for the proposed garden, or you could request that they come up with solutions to renovate an existing space. In the design, students would have to consider where paths would be implemented and whether their design was inclusive of all students (Taylor et al., 2021). For example, in a school that caters to students with special needs, the garden paths would have to be wide enough to be wheelchair accessible. Planting beds need to be at an adequate height that is both ergonomically pleasant for students and teachers, but equally easy to reach for younger students. Seating areas need to be shaded, but not somewhere that will likely be easily soiled (by birds or bats). Any structures that are included in the garden to house tools and other resources have to be robust enough to resist the strong right foot of Bobby playing football not too far from the garden. If these structures are made of glass, they are likely to break easily, which is not ideal in an educational context.

It is important to have a consultation process with students, teachers, parents and the community so that everyone feels invested in the school garden and that it accurately reflects your community – remember, one of the key factors of school garden success is that it has a community identity and involvement. Then let the creativity roll on – design the garden in line with whatever it is that your community wants it to be.

Choose plants that are suitable for your climate, soil and the garden's purpose. Consider native plants to support local biodiversity. Additionally, you may like to incorporate elements such as sensory zones, space for Yarning Circles or vertical gardens based on the specific needs and cultural context of your school. Provide deep consideration of your local context – who are your stakeholders, how do they use the garden, and does the garden represent their identity?

STEP 4: Secure funding and resources

Finding the appropriate funding for your school garden can prove challenging. It is important to get all key stakeholders involved and request that people use their networks and skills to raise the important funds needed for the implementation and maintenance of the school garden. Retirees in your local community may be ex-professionals with extensive writing experience. Put that to good use by kindly asking them if they could help you apply for grants from the local government, non-profit organisations and businesses. One school I visited was awarded a $35,000 Queensland Government Gambling Fund Grant to renovate their school garden. It went a long way to creating not only an amazing school garden, but an entire kitchen facility for the children to prepare and cook the produce that they had harvested. So, reach out to the community – the skills that you are looking for will exist!

Seeking donations is also a great way to raise some funds. Ask local businesses to donate funds or supplies to get the garden up and running. You can also do fundraising events – outdoor cinemas, bake sales, car washing or crowdfunding. Get the community involved by publishing your fundraising endeavours on the local community social media pages or at local libraries and shopping centres (you'd be surprised how many people read the noticeboard as they pack their groceries).

STEP 5: Implement

Then starts your implementation! Clear the site by removing any debris, weeds, invasive trees or older structures from the site. Improve the soil by preparing it with organic compost – local organisations or volunteer associations (or quite simply your community garden) might be able to help with this part. Build the structures and the beds according to a preapproved plan.

Get everyone involved in the garden's creation and implementation. You can integrate the garden into all subject areas – science, maths, art and social studies – include a five-minute workshop on this at each staff meeting. Have guest speakers and offer PD for your teachers, parents and students on anything that is even remotely peripheral to the garden. Host these sessions within or around the garden space when possible.

STEP 6: Maintain and sustain

Create a schedule of events and allocate specific times when people (students, teachers, parents, community members) can enter the garden – this may mean that the community can enter on a Monday from 3.30pm to 5.30pm when students have gone home or 5am to 7.30am before students arrive at school. Then, just maintain and sustain, planning regular tasks to keep the garden active and thriving.

Importantly, track the progress of your garden by keeping records of what is planted and harvested, and any challenges faced so that the knowledge is there long after you have left your role as a teacher.

STEP 7: Reflect and adapt

Regularly evaluate your objectives and those of your community. Regularly assess whether your goals and objectives are being met and adjust plans as needed. Celebrate successes – this may be through community events such as harvest festivals, hosting events in the garden to show and share produce, demonstrating the hard work of the teachers, parents, students and community members or using the newsletter to share stories. Events and stories can also be shared on social media, in the school newsletter and at school assemblies to let everyone know how *good* the school garden is and how important it is to the community.

Make sure you reflect and adapt – it is critical that the school garden remains dynamic and evolutionary. Collect feedback from students, teachers, parents and community members about the garden's impact and areas for improvement. Make necessary adjustments to improve the garden based on feedback and ongoing evaluations.

And, over time, expand programs. Look for new opportunities to integrate the garden into more aspects of school and community life.

By following this structured plan, you can create a school garden that not only provides health and wellbeing benefits but also serves as a powerful tool for community engagement, educational enrichment and personal growth for students. Remember, the success of a school garden relies on the active involvement and support of the entire school community, tailored to the unique sociocultural context of your school.

CONCLUSION

As we reach the end of this journey through the complex and stimulating world of school gardens, I hope you've found inspiration and practical guidance to bring these enriching spaces to your own school. The transformative power of school gardens is immense, offering far more than just nutritional benefits. These gardens provide a dynamic and multifaceted learning environment that can deeply impact our students' lives.

In a society where children have increasingly limited access to nature spaces due to challenges with time and proximity, school gardens have become essential. They provide a safe and semistructured yet flexible environment where children can explore, learn and grow. By integrating school gardens into your teaching, we can ensure that children feel the interconnectedness of our world. School gardens are not just the next best trend, they are a vital component of a holistic and inclusive education system that prepares the whole child to be a thoughtful, engaged and resilient decision-maker of the future.

Let me take you back to Billy, the curious yet uncertain little child who thought tomatoes came from the supermarket. His innocent remark highlighted a disconnect between children and the natural world – a gap that school gardens can beautifully bridge. Billy's story is not unique; many children today are distanced from the origins of their food and the processes of nature. School gardens reconnect them with these vital aspects, offering hands-on experiences in sustainability, biodiversity and environmental stewardship, but also other rewarding benefits that extend far beyond health and wellbeing.

At your school, maybe the garden's design and activities focus on providing sensory and therapeutic experiences tailored to the specific needs of the students in your care. The structured and secure environment of the garden helped manage behaviours and provide a calming space, crucial for the students' emotional and behavioural development. This therapeutic approach directly responds to the sociocultural context of your school, highlighting the importance of creating educational spaces that address the unique needs of your diverse student populations.

Or maybe your school garden will focus on fostering a deep connection to community and heritage. By engaging students in practical skills such as planting and harvesting, the garden can promote physical activity and instil a sense of pride and accomplishment. This space may be a symbol of the community's values and traditions, reinforcing the students' sense of identity and belonging.

A school garden can be a unique green oasis within a concrete or urban space. At your school, students could engage in informal interactions, develop social skills and gain environmental awareness all through their interactions with and within the school garden. The garden's role in supporting student wellbeing may be closely tied to the sociocultural context of the urban community, where environmental education and sustainability are prioritised.

These examples demonstrate that school gardens are not just about growing plants – they are about growing minds, relationships and communities. They can be therapeutic spaces that fulfil sensory needs, promote physical activity and develop practical skills. They help students understand where their food comes from and they foster a sense of responsibility towards nature. They help us to build communities, and build ourselves as individuals and enhance our sense of belonging.

As teachers, we should make the effort to integrate school gardens into our educational practices because these spaces support our students' holistic development. By creating interactive and inclusive learning experiences, school gardens cater to diverse student needs and promote a well-rounded educational and recreational approach. School gardens are nutritional, therapeutic, physical, practical, emotional, social and academic spaces in educational settings.

This book has shown that the benefits of school gardens are multifaceted. They offer therapeutic and sensory benefits, create calming environments and engage students in physical activities. They also play a significant role in developing practical skills and enhancing emotional and social wellbeing. Gardens foster peer-to-peer connections, improve student-teacher relationships, and provide a safe and secure environment for exploration and learning. Integrating garden activities into the curriculum enriches academic learning, making subjects such as science, maths and art come to life through real-world applications.

To maximise the benefits of school gardens, it is essential to understand the sociocultural context of each school and tailor garden programs to meet specific needs. This book encourages you to reflect on your practices, celebrate your successes and continuously adapt your approaches. Embrace the curiosity, flexibility and commitment to continuous improvement that will allow you to create enriching, sustainable and impactful educational experiences for your students.

In chapter 2 I described the joy I felt bringing that little plant into my school garden in Year 1 in Toowoomba. Its soft, furry texture and the pride I felt in sharing it with my friends created a lasting memory. To this day, rubbing lavender flowers between my fingers and inhaling their fragrance brings me immense joy and reminds me of our interconnectedness with the world around us. This is the kind of lasting impact a school garden can have. Perhaps you have similar memories you can draw upon.

As we conclude, I encourage you to embrace the myriad benefits of school gardens and advocate for their integration into your educational practices. By starting and maintaining a school garden, you will create enriching, dynamic and inclusive learning environments that cater to the diverse needs of your students. You will foster a greater sense of interconnectedness and stewardship towards the world around us.

From one teacher who loves her students to another, let's make our gardens grow, and in doing so, watch our students blossom.

ACTION PLAN

By following this comprehensive action plan, you can create a school garden that not only provides health and wellbeing benefits but also serves as a powerful tool for community engagement, educational enrichment and personal growth for students. The success of a school garden relies on the active involvement and support of the entire school community, tailored to the unique sociocultural context of your school.

STEP 1: Initial planning and assessment

Assess current situation:

- [ ] Identify existing garden spaces or the need to create new ones.
- [ ] Evaluate available tools and resources.
- [ ] Determine the condition of resources such as tools and garden beds.
- [ ] Understand potential stakeholders and their roles.

Set goals and objectives:

- [ ] Define the purpose of the school garden: educational purposes, community-building, promoting sustainability and therapeutic space.
- [ ] Use the SMART framework (specific, measurable, achievable, relevant, time-bound) to set clear objectives.

Conduct a site analysis:

- [ ] Assess soil quality, sunlight exposure, water availability and space constraints.

- [ ] Address safety and security measures to ensure the garden is a safe space for all students.
- [ ] Identify potential hazards and ensure proper planning to address these issues.

STEP 2: Engage the community and gather support

Identify support networks:

- [ ] Engage other teachers, parents and community members in supporting the garden.
- [ ] Identify champions within the community who can take on leadership roles.

Host community meetings:

- [ ] Share the vision and plans for the school garden.
- [ ] Gather input and ideas from the community to ensure the garden meets their needs and expectations.
- [ ] Build enthusiasm and encourage community involvement.

Create roles and responsibilities:

- [ ] Assign roles such as project manager, fundraiser, garden coordinator and communication lead.
- [ ] Encourage participants to self-elect into roles that align with their interests and skills.

STEP 3: Design the garden

Engage students in the design process:

- [ ] Use the design of the school garden as an educational activity for upper primary students.
- [ ] Consider inclusivity, such as wheelchair accessibility and age-appropriate garden bed heights.

Develop a comprehensive garden plan:

- ☐ Design the layout of the garden, including paths, planting beds, seating areas and structures.
- ☐ Choose plants suitable for the climate and soil, focusing on native plants to support local biodiversity.

Consider cultural context:

- ☐ Ensure the garden reflects the cultural heritage and identity of the school community.
- ☐ Incorporate elements such as sensory gardens, Yarning Circles and vertical gardens based on community needs.

STEP 4: Secure funding and resources

Apply for grants and seek donations:

- ☐ Identify grants from local government, non-profit organisations and businesses.
- ☐ Reach out to local businesses for donations of funds or supplies.
- ☐ Host fundraising events such as outdoor cinemas, bake sales or car washes.

Involve the community in fundraising:

- ☐ Utilise community members' skills and networks to support fundraising efforts.
- ☐ Publicise fundraising efforts on community social media pages, local libraries and shopping centres.

STEP 5: Implement

Prepare the site:

- ☐ Clear debris, weeds and older structures.

- [ ] Improve soil quality with organic compost.
- [ ] Build structures and planting beds according to the approved plan.

Involve the community in implementation:

- [ ] Host community events and working bees to involve students, teachers, parents and community members in the garden's creation and maintenance.

Integrate the garden into the curriculum:

- [ ] Develop lesson plans that incorporate the garden into science, maths, art and social studies.
- [ ] Use the garden as a space for experiential learning and skill development.

STEP 6: Maintain and sustain

Schedule regular maintenance:

- [ ] Plan regular tasks to keep the garden active and thriving.
- [ ] Assign responsibilities for maintenance tasks to students, teachers and community volunteers.

Track progress and evaluate:

- [ ] Keep records of what is planted, harvested and any challenges faced.
- [ ] Regularly assess whether goals and objectives are being met and adjust plans as needed.

Celebrate successes:

- [ ] Host community events such as harvest festivals to showcase the garden's achievements.
- [ ] Share stories and updates about the garden in the school newsletter, on social media and at school assemblies.

STEP 7: Reflect and adapt

Collect feedback:

☐ Gather input from students, teachers, parents and community members about the garden's impact and areas for improvement.

Make necessary adjustments:

☐ Use feedback and ongoing evaluations to make improvements to the garden.

Expand programs:

☐ Look for new opportunities to integrate the garden into more aspects of school and community life.

REFERENCES

Ahmed, S. M., Lemkau, J. P., Nealeigh, N., & Mann, B. (2011). Barriers to healthcare access in a non-elderly urban poor American population. *Health & Social Care in the Community, 9*(6), 445-453.

Akerlof, K., Maibach, E. W., Fitzgerald, D., Cedeno, A. Y., & Neuman, A. (2013). Do people "personally experience" global warming, and if so how, and does it matter? Global Environmental Change, 23(1), 81-91. https://doi.org/10.1016/j.gloenvcha.2012.07.006

Alexander, J., North, M. W., & Hendren, D. K. (1995). Master gardener classroom garden project: An evaluation of the benefits to children. *Children's Environments, 12*(2), 123-133.

Anderson, M. (2017). Place-based education: Connecting classroom and community. *Education and Urban Society, 49*(3), 205-229.

Andersson, K., & Borg, K. (2023). School gardens and inclusivity: Examining the hidden curriculum. *Educational Research Review, 29*, 100383.

Antonovsky, A. (1987). *Unraveling the mystery of health: How people manage stress and stay well*. Jossey-Bass.

Australian Curriculum Assessment and Reporting Authority. (2019). Australian Curriculum: Health and Physical Education. https://www.australiancurriculum.edu.au

Australian Curriculum Assessment and Reporting Authority. (2023a). Australian Curriculum: Health and Physical Education. https://www.australiancurriculum.edu.au

Australian Curriculum Assessment and Reporting Authority. (2023b). Australian Curriculum: Sustainability. https://www.australiancurriculum.edu.au

Australian Education for Sustainability Alliance. (2014). *Enablers for Lasting School Change*. https://www.educationforsustainability.org.au

Berto, R. (2014). The role of nature in coping with psycho-physiological stress: A literature review on restorativeness. *Behavioral Sciences, 4*(4), 394-409.

Blair, D. (2009). The child in the garden: An evaluative review of the benefits of school gardening. *Journal of Environmental Education, 40*(2), 15-38.

Blanchet-Cohen, N., & Elliot, E. (2011). Young children and educators engagement and learning outdoors: A basis for rights-based programming. *Early Education and Development, 22*(5), 757-777.

Block, K., Gibbs, L., Staiger, P. K., Gold, L., Johnson, B., Macfarlane, S., & Waters, E. (2012). Growing community: The impact of the Stephanie Alexander Kitchen Garden Program on the social and learning environment in primary schools. *Health Education & Behavior, 39*(4), 419-432.

Bowker, R., & Tearle, P. (2007). Gardening as a learning environment: A study of children's perceptions and understanding of school gardens as part of an international project. *Learning Environments Research, 10*(2), 83-100.

Buch, E. (2006). The role of stress in the relationships between work and family. *Journal of Occupational Health Psychology, 11*(2), 169-181.

Burt, K. G., Koch, P., & Contento, I. R. (2018). Development of the GREEN tool: Green tool for reliable evaluation of school gardens. *Journal of Nutrition Education and Behavior, 50*(4), 394-400.

Capaldi, C. A., Passmore, H. A., Nisbet, E. K., Zelenski, J. M., & Dopko, R. L. (2014). Flourishing in nature: A review of the benefits of connecting with nature and its application as a well-being intervention. *International Journal of Wellbeing, 5*(4), 1-16.

Chawla, L. (2009). Childhood experiences associated with care for the natural world: A theoretical framework for empirical results. *Children, Youth and Environments, 17*(4), 144-170.

Chawla, L. (2014). Children's engagement with the natural world as a ground for healing and hope. In A. C. Blazek & P. G. Cohen (Eds.), *The Handbook of Global Childhoods* (pp. 38-56). Springer.

Chawla, L., Keena, K., Pevec, I., & Stanley, E. (2014). Green schoolyards as havens from stress and resources for resilience in childhood and adolescence. *Health & Place, 28*, 1-13.

Chiumento, A., Machin, L., & Taylor, M. (2018). School gardens and student well-being: A heuristic review. *Health & Place, 52*, 10-20.

Christian, M. S., Evans, C. E., Hancock, N., & Nykjaer, C. (2014). Family meals can help children reach their 5 A Day: An analysis of children's fruit and vegetable intake from the National Diet and Nutrition Survey (2008–2011). *Public Health Nutrition, 17*(7), 1509-1518.

Cohen, S., & Jimenez, M. (2008). Sensory integration: Addressing the needs of all students in school gardens. *Journal of Child Health Care, 12*(1), 35-42.

Connelly, J., Markey, S., & Roseland, M. (2012). We know enough: Achieving action through the convergence of sustainable community development and the social economy. *Economy and Society, 41*(4), 496-523.

Coomber, N. (2022). Decolonizing school gardens: Inclusion of Aboriginal agricultural practices in Australian schools. *Indigenous Education Journal, 14*(3), 245-260.

Corraliza, J. A., Collado, S., & Bethelmy, L. (2012). Nature as a moderator of stress in urban children. *Social Indicators Research, 110*(3), 1-16.

Cutter-Mackenzie, A. (2009). Multicultural school gardens: Creating engaging garden spaces in learning about language, culture, and environment. *Environmental Education Research, 15*(4), 523-539.

Danks, S. G. (2010). *Asphalt to Ecosystems: Design Ideas for Schoolyard Transformation.* New Village Press.

Davis, B. L., Valcan, D. S., & Pino-Pasternak, D. (2021). Executive function and self-regulated learning in Australian children: A study of associations and predictors. *Journal of Educational Psychology, 113*(2), 303-320.

Department of Education and Training. (2023). Early Years Learning Framework. https://www.dese.gov.au/early-years-learning-framework

Depledge, M. H., Stone, R. J., & Bird, W. J. (2019). Can natural and virtual environments be used to promote improved human health and wellbeing? *Environmental Science & Technology, 43*(5), 280-284.

Devine, C. M. (2005). A life course perspective: Understanding food choices in time, social location, and history. *Journal of Nutrition Education and Behavior, 37*(3), 121-128.

Dring, M., Elliott, S., & Forbes, C. (2020). School gardens as spaces for outdoor learning and development: A systematic review. *International Journal of Environmental Research and Public Health, 17*(15), 5456.

Dyment, J. E., & Bell, A. C. (2008). Grounds for movement: Green school grounds as sites for promoting physical activity. *Health Education Research, 23*(6), 952-962.

Eames-Sheavly, M. (1994). A school garden program as a context for teaching standard-based science. *Journal of Extension, 32*(2), 1-7.

Education in Emergencies UNICEF. (2020). The role of education in peacebuilding and conflict prevention. https://www.unicef.org/education/emergencies

Edwards-Jones, A., Waite, S., & Passy, R. (2018). Falling into LINE: School strategies for overcoming challenges associated with learning in natural environments (LINE). *Education 3-13, 46*(1), 49-63.

Elliott, E. (2010). Participatory action research: Challenges, complications, and opportunities. *Public Health Nursing, 27*(2), 142-148.

Falk, J. H., Dierking, L. D., & Adams, M. (2001). Situating cognition: The role of place in the development of thought. *Journal of Educational Psychology, 93*(2), 141-148.

Fieldhouse, J. (2003). The impact of an allotment group on mental health clients' health, wellbeing, and social networking. *British Journal of Occupational Therapy, 66*(7), 286-296.

Firth, C., Maye, D., & Pearson, D. (2011). Developing 'community' in community gardens. *Local Environment, 16*(6), 555-568.

Fischer, K. (2018). Barriers to implementing outdoor learning in primary schools: A case study of a local authority in England. *Education 3-13, 46*(1), 49-63.

Fjørtoft, I., & Sageie, J. (2000). The natural environment as a playground for children: Landscape description and analyses of a natural landscape. *Landscape and Urban Planning, 48*(1-2), 83-97.

Fuller, R. A., Irvine, K. N., Devine-Wright, P., Warren, P. H., & Gaston, K. J. (2010). Psychological benefits of greenspace increase with biodiversity. *Biology Letters, 3*(4), 390-394.

Gandini, L. (1998). Educational and caring spaces. In C. Edwards, L. Gandini, & G. Forman (Eds.), *The hundred languages of children: The Reggio Emilia approach—Advanced reflections* (2nd ed., pp. 161-178). Ablex Publishing.

Garitsis, C. (2016). School gardens and experiential learning: A study of student engagement in primary school gardens. *Journal of Environmental Education, 47*(2), 93-105.

Gatto, N. M., Ventura, E. E., Cook, L. T., Gyllenhammer, L. E., & Davis, J. N. (2017). LA Sprouts: A garden-based nutrition intervention pilot program influences motivation and preferences for fruits and vegetables in Latino youth. *Journal of the Academy of Nutrition and Dietetics, 107*(3), 489-500.

Giusti, M., Barthel, S., & Marcus, L. (2014). Nature routines and affinity with the biosphere: A case study of preschool children in Stockholm. *Children, Youth and Environments, 24*(3), 16-42.

Goodall, J. (2016). Learning beyond the classroom: Education for a changing world. *International Journal of Educational Research, 76*, 15-24.

Graves, J. E., Hughes, K. J., & Bower, J. M. (2016). The impact of school gardens on children's STEM education. *Journal of Science Education and Technology, 25*(4), 576-589.

Greer, M. L., Yoder, N. L., & Levenson, A. (2019). Teacher engagement in school gardens: A framework for understanding success and failure. *Journal of Environmental Education, 50*(1), 32-45.

Hammel, K. W. (2004). Dimensions of meaning in the occupations of daily life. *Canadian Journal of Occupational Therapy, 71*(5), 296-305.

Heffernan, A., Bright, D., & Kim, M. (2019). The status of teachers and the teaching profession: A survey of Australian public perceptions. *Australian Journal of Education, 63*(1), 43-60.

Henryks, J. (2011). Growing community: Starting and nurturing community gardens. *Community Development Journal, 46*(3), 483-485.

Herbst, C. M. (2022). Child care in the United States: Markets, policy, and evidence. *Journal of Policy Analysis and Management, 42*(1), 255-304.

Herzog, T. R. (2002). A cognitive analysis of preference for waterscapes. *Journal of Environmental Psychology, 9*(3), 225-241.

Inzlicht, M., Werner, K. M., Briskin, J. L., & Roberts, B. W. (2021). Integrating models of self-regulation. *Annual Review of Psychology, 72*, 319-347.

James, A. (2007). Children, media and health in the digital age. *Children & Society, 21*(2), 70-80.

Jana, M. (2018). School gardens: A sustainable approach to build positive learning environments. *International Journal of Environmental Research and Public Health, 15*(7), 1532.

Jones, M., Dailami, N., Weitkamp, E., Salmon, D., Kimberlee, R., Morley, A., & Orme, J. (2012). Food sustainability education as a route to healthier eating: Evaluation of a multi-component school programme in English primary schools. *Health Education Research, 27*(3), 448-458.

Kabat-Zinn, J. (2005). *Coming to Our Senses: Healing Ourselves and the World Through Mindfulness*. Hyperion.

Kals, E., Schumacher, D., & Montada, L. (1999). Emotional affinity toward nature as a motivational basis to protect nature. *Environment and Behavior, 31*(2), 178-202.

Kaplan, R., & Kaplan, S. (1989). *The Experience of Nature: A Psychological Perspective*. Cambridge University Press.

Kararo, M. J., Simon, A. L., & Blalock, L. B. (2016). Using a school garden program to foster high school students' environmental literacy and stewardship. *Journal of Environmental Education, 47*(2), 104-117.

Keeler, R. (2008). *Natural playscapes: Creating outdoor play environments for the soul*. Exchange Press.

Keniger, L. E., Gaston, K. J., Irvine, K. N., & Fuller, R. A. (2013). What are the benefits of interacting with nature? *International Journal of Environmental Research and Public Health, 10*(3), 913-935.

Kim, L. E., Asbury, K., & McMahon, T. (2022). Teacher stress and burnout during COVID-19: A qualitative study in England. *Educational Psychology, 42*(8), 1036-1053.

Kingsley, J. Y., Townsend, M., & Henderson-Wilson, C. (2019). Cultivating health and wellbeing: Members' perceptions of the health benefits of a Port Melbourne community garden. *Leisure Studies, 38*(3), 345-359.

Knorr, D., Khoo, C., & Augustin, M. A. (2018). Food for an Urban Planet: Challenges and Research Opportunities. *Frontiers in Nutrition, 5*(73).

Koch, S., Waliczek, T. M., & Zajicek, J. M. (2006). The effect of a summer garden program on the nutritional knowledge, attitudes, and behaviors of children. *HortTechnology, 16*(4), 620-625.

Kuo, F. E. (2001). Coping with poverty: Impacts of environment and attention in the inner city. *Environment and Behavior, 33*(1), 5-34.

Landry, M. J., van den Berg, A. E., Hoelscher, D. M., & Estabrooks, P. A. (2021). Impact of a school garden intervention on dietary behaviors and physical activity in elementary school children. *Journal of School Health, 91*(1), 23-32.

Larson, L. R., & Miller, K. (2011). Ethnic variation in the perceptions of wildlife and experiences in nature. *Journal of Environmental Psychology, 31*(4), 401-410.

Lin, B. B., Fuller, R. A., Bush, R., Gaston, K. J., & Shanahan, D. F. (2018). Opportunity or orientation? Who uses urban parks and why. *PLOS ONE, 9*(1), e87022.

Lineberger, S. E., & Zajicek, J. M. (2000). School gardens: Can a hands-on teaching tool affect students' attitudes and behaviors regarding fruit and vegetables? *HortTechnology, 10*(3), 593-597.

Lochner, L. (2019). Colonial legacies in Australian school gardens: A historical perspective. *Australian Journal of Education, 63*(2), 164-179.

Loftus, J. E., Richardson, M., & Thompson, J. (2017). The future of green space: Lessons from Los Angeles. *Urban Forestry & Urban Greening, 22*, 74-83.

Louv, R. (2008). *Last Child in the Woods: Saving Our Children from Nature-Deficit Disorder.* Algonquin Books.

Lozzi, D. (1989). Community gardens: Policy and practice in the United States. *Journal of Urban Affairs, 11*(2), 45-56.

Lucke, J. F., Grossman, E. R., & Lipschitz, J. M. (2019). Social connectedness in a school-based gardening program. *Journal of Child and Family Studies, 28*(6), 1672-1684.

Lupinacci, J., Craig, J., & Lemke, L. (2022). Gender roles in school gardens: An intersectional analysis. *Gender and Education, 34*(3), 345-362.

Mackay, C. M., & Schmitt, M. T. (2019). Do people who feel connected to nature do more to protect it? A meta-analysis. *Journal of Environmental Psychology, 65*, 101323.

Maller, C. J. (2005). Hands-on contact with nature in primary schools as a catalyst for developing a sense of community and well-being. *Australasian Journal of Environmental Education, 21*, 37-48.

Marchant, G., Zajicek, J., & Hegwood, C. (2019). School gardens: Teaching students and building communities. *Journal of Extension, 57*(2), 1-10.

Meiselman, H. L. (2016). Quality of life, well-being and wellness: Measuring subjective health for foods and other products. *Food Quality and Preference, 37*, 31-40.

Miller, D. L. (2007). The seeds of learning: Young children develop important skills through their gardening activities at a Midwestern early education program. *Applied Environmental Education & Communication, 6*(1), 49-66.

Miller, J. R., Hobbs, R. J., & Smith, F. P. (2009). Evaluating the importance of ecological context when planning restoration. *Restoration Ecology, 17*(6), 586-591.

Mittelmark, M. B., Bull, T., & Vaandrager, L. (2016). The salutogenic model of health: The role of generalized resistance resources. In M. B. Mittelmark, S. Sagy, M. Eriksson, G. F. Bauer, J. M. Pelikan, B. Lindström, & G. A. Espnes (Eds.), *The Handbook of Salutogenesis* (pp. 95-106). Springer.

Mittelmark, M. B., Bull, T., & Vaandrager, L. (2022). Understanding salutogenesis: The role of generalized resistance resources. In M. B. Mittelmark, S. Sagy, M. Eriksson, G. F. Bauer, J. M. Pelikan, B. Lindström, & G. A. Espnes (Eds.), *Global Perspectives on Health Promotion Effectiveness* (pp. 107-117). Springer.

Moore, R. C., & Cooper-Marcus, C. (2008). Healthy planet, healthy children: Designing nature into the daily spaces of childhood. *Biophilic Design: The Theory, Science and Practice of Bringing Buildings to Life*, 153-203.

Moore, R., & Young, D. (1978). Childhood outdoors: Toward a social ecology of the landscape. In I. Altman & J. F. Wohlwill (Eds.), *Children and the Environment* (pp. 83-130). Springer.

Moore, R., Lange, M., & Oates, R. (2021). Concrete playgrounds: The impact of urban environments on children's outdoor play. *Urban Studies, 58*(3), 550-565.

Mujis, D., & Bokhove, C. (2020). Self-regulation in learning: The role of motivational beliefs. *Educational Psychology Review, 32*(2), 479-507.

Musek, J., & Polic, M. (2014). The structure of self-rated health and the structure of well-being. *Personality and Individual Differences, 66*, 135-140.

Musich, S., Wang, S. S., Hawkins, K., & Yeh, C. S. (2018). The impact of spirituality and religion on well-being in the elderly. *Geriatric Nursing, 39*(6), 653-664.

Nicol, R. (2020). Outdoor education: Research summary. *International Journal of Primary, Elementary and Early Years Education, 45*(4), 371-382.

Nisbet, E. K., Zelenski, J. M., & Murphy, S. A. (2009). The nature relatedness scale: Linking individuals' connection with nature to environmental concern and behavior. *Environment and Behavior, 41*(5), 715-740.

Ohly, H., Gentry, S., Wigglesworth, R., Bethel, A., Lovell, R., & Garside, R. (2016). A systematic review of the health and well-being impacts of school gardening: Synthesis of quantitative and qualitative evidence. *BMC Public Health, 16*(286).

Okely, T., Sumner, R., & Hillman, M. (2021). School gardens: A systematic review of interventions and outcomes. *Health Promotion International, 36*(5), 121-133.

Okiror, J. J., Matsiko, F. B., & Ssempebwa, J. (2011). School gardens: Promoting STEM education through experiential learning. *Educational Research and Reviews, 6*(14), 891-897.

Ong, L., West, S. E., & Kingsley, J. (2019). Understanding a community garden as a therapeutic landscape. *Health & Place, 55*, 132-143.

Oulton, R., & Jagger, S. (2023). Colonialist perspectives in school garden research and their impact on Indigenous student inclusion. *Journal of Environmental Education, 54*(1), 45-60.

Papadopoulou, P., Lagoudaki, R., & Andreou, E. (2020). Promoting child health through school gardening programs: A review. *Journal of Health Education Research & Development, 38*(2), 201-211.

Passy, R., Morris, M., & Reed, F. (2010). *Impact of school gardening on learning: Final report*. National Foundation for Educational Research. https://www.nfer.ac.uk/publications/SGAR01

Petersson, K. (2022). Sensory-friendly school gardens: Designing for all students. *Landscape Research, 47*(2), 225-239.

Popkin, B. M., Duffey, K., & Gordon-Larsen, P. (2005). Environmental influences on food choice, physical activity and energy balance. *Physiology & Behavior, 86*(5), 603-613.

Pritchard, A., Richardson, M., Sheffield, D., & McEwan, K. (2020). The relationship between nature connectedness and eudaimonic well-being: A meta-analysis. *Journal of Happiness Studies, 21*(3), 1145-1167.

Rees, A., & Melix, J. (2019). Urban gardening in schools: Challenges and opportunities for inclusive education. *Urban Education, 54*(10), 1407-1424.

Richardson, L. (1994). Writing: A method of inquiry. In N. K. Denzin & Y. S. Lincoln (Eds.), *Handbook of qualitative research* (pp. 516-529). Sage Publications.

Richardson, M., Hallam, J., & Lumber, R. (2016). One thousand good things in nature: Aspects of nearby nature associated with improved connection to nature. *Environmental Values, 25*(5), 605-624.

Robinson, C. W., & Zajicek, J. M. (2005). Growing minds: The effect of a one-year school garden program on six constructs of life skills of elementary school children. *HortTechnology, 15*(3), 453-457.

Rowles, G. D. (2008). Place in occupational science: A life course perspective on the role of environmental context in the quest for meaning. *Journal of Occupational Science, 15*(3), 127-135.

Sahrakhiz, S., Harring, M., & Witte, K. (2018). Learning in nature: A review of the field. *Educational Research Review, 25,* 1-9.

Schwab, K. (2015). The Fourth Industrial Revolution: What it means and how to respond. *Foreign Affairs, 95*(6), 1-11.

Shepard, P. (2009). *Nature and madness.* University of Georgia Press.

Skår, M., & Krogh, E. (2009). Changes in children's nature-based experiences near home: From spontaneous play to adult-controlled, planned and organized activities. *Children's Geographies, 7*(3), 339-354.

Skelly, S. M., & Zajicek, J. M. (1998). The effect of an interdisciplinary garden program on the environmental attitudes of elementary school students. *HortTechnology, 8*(4), 579-583.

Sobel, D. (2008). *Children and nature: Design principles for educators.* Stenhouse Publishers.

Somerset, S., Ball, R., Flett, M., & Geissman, R. (2005). School-based community gardens: Re-establishing healthy relationships with food. *Journal of the Home Economics Institute of Australia, 12*(2), 25-33.

Stoltz, K. B., & Schaffer, A. (2018). Stress and well-being in the workplace: A salutogenic approach to occupational health. *Journal of Occupational Health Psychology, 23*(2), 247-259.

Taylor, A. F., Kuo, F. E., & Sullivan, W. C. (2001). Coping with ADD: The surprising connection to green play settings. *Environment and Behavior, 33*(1), 54-77.

Taylor, K., van den Berg, L., Lansigan, R. K., & Iyer, P. (2021). Children's experience and perception of school gardens: A systematic review and case study. *International Journal of Environmental Research and Public Health, 18*(2), 725.

Teig, E., Amulya, J., Bardwell, L., Buchenau, M., Marshall, J. A., & Litt, J. S. (2009). Collective efficacy in Denver, Colorado: Strengthening neighborhoods and health through community gardens. *Health & Place, 15*(4), 1115-1122.

Truong, J., Thompson, J., & Loftus, J. E. (2022). Reimagining green spaces in urban areas: A case study of Sydney. *Landscape and Urban Planning, 220,* 104-112.

Turner, L., Sandoval, A., & Chaloupka, F. J. (2014). School garden programs: An evaluation of the benefits for children and communities. *Journal of Nutrition Education and Behavior, 46*(4), 267-273.

Twohig-Bennett, C., & Jones, A. (2018). The health benefits of the great outdoors: A systematic review and meta-analysis of greenspace exposure and health outcomes. *Environmental Research, 166,* 628-637.

Ulrich, R. S. (1993). Biophilia, biophobia, and natural landscapes. In S. R. Kellert & E. O. Wilson (Eds.), *The Biophilia Hypothesis* (pp. 73-137). Island Press.

United Nations. (2018). *World Urbanization Prospects: The 2018 Revision.* Department of Economic and Social Affairs, Population Division. https://population.un.org/wup/Publications/Files/WUP2018-Report.pdf

Van Dijk-Wesselius, J. E., Maas, J., Hovinga, D., van Vugt, M., & van den Berg, A. E. (2018). The impact of school gardens on children's physical activity and mental health. Urban Forestry & Urban Greening, 28, 25-30. https://doi.org/10.1016/j.ufug.2017.12.007

Van Dijk-Wesselius, J. E., Maas, J., Hovinga, D., van Vugt, M., & van den Berg, A. E. (2020). The impact of greening schoolyards on the appreciation, physical activity, and health of school children: A prospective intervention study. *Landscape and Urban Planning, 202,* 103116.

Veen, E. J., Bock, B. B., van den Berg, W., Visser, A. J., & Wiskerke, J. S. C. (2016). Community gardening and social cohesion: Different designs, different motivations. *Local Environment, 21*(10), 1271-1287.

Veitch, J., Bagley, S., Ball, K., & Salmon, J. (2006). Where do children usually play? A qualitative study of parents' perceptions of influences on children's active free-play. *Health & Place, 12*(4), 383-393.

Vinje, H. F., Langeland, E., & Bull, T. (2017). Living the good life: A meta-synthesis of qualitative studies on well-being in retirement. *Scandinavian Journal of Public Health, 45*(2), 150-162.

Viola, A. (2006). Evaluation of the Outreach School Garden Project: Building the capacity of two Indigenous remote school communities to integrate nutrition into the core school curriculum. *Health Promotion Journal of Australia, 17*(3), 233-239.

Wagner, B. J., Latimer, L. A., Adams, C. A., & Carmichael-Olson, H. (2020). Executive function and self-regulated learning in young children: Examining interrelations and predictors of growth over time. *Journal of Educational Psychology, 112*(2), 283-298.

Waliczek, T. M., Bradley, J. C., & Zajicek, J. M. (2001). The effect of school gardens on children's interpersonal relationships and attitudes toward school. *HortTechnology, 11*(3), 466-468.

Warshaw, J., & Bolderman, C. (2008). A garden in every school: A study of school garden programs in Alameda County. *California Agriculture, 62*(1), 27-31.

Watts, N., Adger, W. N., Ayeb-Karlsson, S., Bai, Y., Byass, P., Campbell-Lendrum, D.,... & Costello, A. (2015). The Lancet Countdown: Tracking progress on health and climate change. *The Lancet, 386*(10007), 1861-1914.

Wei, J. (2012). School gardens as learning spaces: Enhancing environmental literacy through experiential learning. *International Journal of Environmental and Science Education, 7*(3), 561-578.

West, J. (2022). The role of school gardens in promoting physical activity and healthy eating among children. *International Journal of Environmental Research and Public Health, 19*(4), 2102.

Wethington, E. (2005). An overview of the life course perspective: Implications for health and nutrition. *Journal of Nutrition Education and Behavior, 37*(3), 115-120.

Whatley, E., Fortune, T., & Williams, A. E. (2015). Enabling factors in community gardening. *British Journal of Occupational Therapy, 78*(6), 398-405.

Whitehead, M. (2018). Cultivating engagement: The educational potential of school gardens. *Educational Research Review, 24*, 10-23.

Williams, D. R. (2006). On and off the 'net: Scales for social capital in an electronic context. *New Media & Society, 8*(3), 459-478.

Williams, D. R., & Dixon, P. S. (2013). Impact of garden-based learning on academic outcomes and motivation in school children: A systematic review. *Review of Educational Research*, 83(2), 211-235.

Wilson, E. O. (2012). *The social conquest of earth.* Liveright Publishing.

Wolsey, T. D., & Lapp, D. (2014). School gardens: The effects on students. *California Reader, 47*(4), 22-29.

Wright, E. O. (2004). *Interrogating inequality: Essays on class analysis, socialism, and Marxism.* Verso.

Yanow, D. (2006). *How does a policy mean? Interpreting policy and organizational actions.* Georgetown University Press.

Yu, S. (2012). Teacher stress and burnout: An international review. *Educational Research, 54*(2), 157-171.

Zimmerman, B. J. (2023). Becoming a self-regulated learner: An overview. *Theory into Practice, 41*(2), 64-70.

www.ingramcontent.com/pod-product-compliance
Lightning Source LLC
Chambersburg PA
CBHW050027130526
44590CB00042B/1987